D0552286

BUDDHISM
ALL THAT MATTERS

467 610 50 2

To Max and Ziggy

BUDDHISM

Pascale
F. Engelmajer

First published in Great Britain in 2013 by Hodder & Stoughton. An Hachette UK company.

First published in US in 2013 by The McGraw-Hill Companies, Inc.

This edition published 2013

Copyright © Pascale F. Engelmajer 2013

The right of Pascale F. Engelmajer to be identified as the Author of the Work has been asserted by her in accordance with the Copyright, Designs and Patents Act 1988.

Database right Hodder & Stoughton (makers)

All rights reserved. No part of this publication may be reproduced, stored in a retrieval system or transmitted in any form or by any means, electronic, mechanical, photocopying, recording or otherwise, without the prior written permission of the publisher, or as expressly permitted by law, or under terms agreed with the appropriate reprographic rights organization. Enquiries concerning reproduction outside the scope of the above should be sent to the Rights Department, Hodder & Stoughton, at the address below.

You must not circulate this book in any other binding or cover and you must impose this same condition on any acquirer.

British Library Cataloguing in Publication Data: a catalogue record for this title is available from the British Library.

Library of Congress Catalog Card Number: on file.

10 9 8 7 6 5 4 3 2 1

The publisher has used its best endeavours to ensure that any website addresses referred to in this book are correct and active at the time of going to press. However, the publisher and the author have no responsibility for the websites and can make no guarantee that a site will remain live or that the content will remain relevant, decent or appropriate.

The publisher has made every effort to mark as such all words which it believes to be trademarks. The publisher should also like to make it clear that the presence of a word in the book, whether marked or unmarked, in no way affects its legal status as a trademark.

Every reasonable effort has been made by the publisher to trace the copyright holders of material in this book. Any errors or omissions should be notified in writing to the publisher, who will endeavour to rectify the situation for any reprints and future editions.

Typeset by Cenveo® Publisher Services.

Printed and bound in Great Britain by CPI Group (UK) Ltd., Croydon, CR0 4YY.

Hodder & Stoughton policy is to use papers that are natural, renewable and recyclable products and made from wood grown in sustainable forests. The logging and manufacturing processes are expected to conform to the environmental regulations of the country of origin.

Hodder & Stoughton Ltd

338 Euston Road

London NW1 3BH

www.hodder.co.uk

Contents

A note on terminology

The Buddhist canon has been preserved in several languages. We do not know what language the Buddha actually spoke, but it is clear from the texts that he avoided the very literate and exclusive Sanskrit to speak the common local languages and encouraged his followers to do the same. The Buddhist texts were first transmitted orally in ancient Indian vernaculars. At some point, they started also being transmitted in Sanskrit, the ancient Indian language of the high caste Brahmins. The Pāli canon as we have it now was committed to written form in the 5th century CE in Sri Lanka in one of these ancient Indian languages. Most of the extant Sanskrit texts were preserved in translations into Chinese and Tibetan, and few original Sanskrit texts have survived the disappearance of Buddhism from its land of birth. When discussing Buddhist ideas, it is almost always necessary to refer to the original Indian terms, as translations into English are mostly inadequate. For example, the concept of *duḥkha* (Pāli: *dukkha*) is always ineffectually rendered whether as 'suffering', 'unsatisfactoriness' or even 'stress'. Indicating the Indian terms therefore ensures that there is no confusion about the concept under discussion. In this volume, when using an English translation, I will initially indicate the original Indian term in brackets with the Sanskrit first and the Pāli second as follows (*duḥkha/dukkha*). Sometimes, I will only use one Indian term indicating, when relevant, the other in parenthesis, as for example: *dukkha* (Skt: *duḥkha*). For non-Indian traditions, I will similarly indicate the original language when relevant.

Introduction

▶ Buddhist morning practices around the world

In Thailand, Ning, a Theravāda Buddhist, lights up a candle and three sticks of incense that she places in front of a Buddha image seated on a carved wooden altar on a wall in her main room. She bows down, placing her hands on the floor near her knees and touching the floor with her forehead, and recites a short prayer. At the end of the prayer, she bows down again three times in sign of respect to the Buddha, the Dharma and the *Saṅgha*. She also regularly sets out fresh flowers on the altar in a small vase.

In Japan, Haruki, a young priest of the Sōtō Zen school, is awakened by the bell at 4.30 a.m. and proceeds to the meditation hall, a long barren room with low wooden benches facing *shoji* screens (paper and wood-frame Japanese walls). Today, it is his turn to carry the *kyōsaku*, the flat stick to keep meditators alert. When the monks are settled down in two rows facing the wall, Haruki walks slowly between them, holding the *kyōsaku* with his two hands in front of him at the level of his stomach. As he walks carefully, he also meditates, focusing on each of his movements, and alert and present to his surroundings.

In Europe, where she is studying for a doctorate, Jin Yen, a Chinese Pure Land Buddhist, also pays her respect to the Buddha before setting out for university. In her monastery, the nuns wake at 4 a.m. and chant for two hours before breakfast. In England, Jin Yen wakes at 5 a.m., and chants and meditates for half an hour before breakfast. She starts by clearing her desk and then offers incense to a small statue of Guanyin a Chinese variation of the Indian Bodhisattva, Avalokiteśvara. She then bows to the Buddha, Dharma and *Saṅgha*, and performs full prostrations to Buddha Amitābha, the Buddha of Pure Land Buddhism, one of the main strands of Buddhism practised in East Asia, before chanting the name of Amitābha, and meditating silently. She ends her meditation by doing some yoga to stretch and rouse herself, and bows again three times.

In North America, Robert starts his day at 6.00 a.m. by first cleaning up around the shrine where he has set up a gilded bronze statue of Tara, a Bodhisattva, photographs of the Dalai Lama and several Tibetan lamas (spiritual teachers), as well as representations of Bodhisattvas and Buddhas. He then sets up bowls filled with water that represent offerings. He is careful to place the bowls in a specific order, close but not touching. At the weekend, when he has time during the day, he uses offerings of water, flowers, incense, light, perfume and food rather than mere water. While he fills and sets the bowls, he recites a short mantra that is believed to help his spiritual practice. Once this is done, he presents the offerings and imagines that they are received by all holy beings, and in particular those placed on his altar.

In these four Buddhist morning practices around the world, the languages, the settings, the statues, the prayers and the nationalities are different. Ning speaks Thai, and makes offerings to a golden statue of the historical Buddha in the main room of her house; Haruki and the monks speak Japanese and meditate in a plain hall; Jin Yen speaks Mandarin Chinese and meditates in front of a beautiful and gentle-featured Chinese Bodhisattva in her monastic cell-like room; Robert speaks English, and prostrates to a colourful and richly adorned Tibetan Bodhisattva in a small shrine room. On the other hand, some aspects are similar: the beings embodied by the statues all originate from ancient India, and even though they have transformed as they travelled through history and countries, they have retained some of their original features. In all Buddhist traditions, respect and worship are demonstrated by bowing down, usually three times, to the Buddha (the teacher), the Dharma (the teachings) and the Saṅgha (the community of disciples), and by presenting offerings of pleasant and pure substances, such as water, flowers, and incense. In addition, every practice usually includes a moment of quiet contemplation, which can last from a few seconds to many hours and even days.

▶ Buddhism in the world

Buddhism was founded around 2,500 years ago by a man called Gotama (Skt: Gautama) in what is today North India. It developed over one and half millennia, spreading to Asia, before it disappeared from its land of origin. As it moved across Asia (see Map 1), different schools and versions took hold, adapting and integrating into the local cultures, while maintaining core ideas and principles.

Today, Buddhists are found on all continents, with the highest concentration in South, Southeast and East Asia.

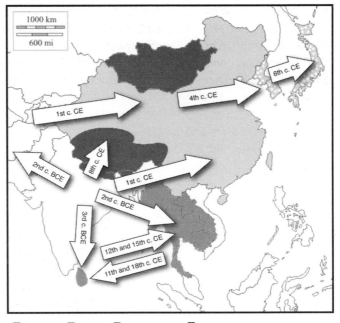

Theravāda ☐ Chinese ☐ Korean-Japanese ■ Tibetan

▲ Figure 0.1 Map 1: The spread of Buddhism in Asia

In this book, we will focus on four fictional characters: Ning, Haruki, Jin Yen and Robert. They represent four of the many expressions of Buddhism: Theravāda Buddhism practised in South and Southeast Asia (Chapter 1), Zen Buddhism practised in Japan (Chapter 2), Pure Land Buddhism practised in East Asia (Chapter 3), and Tibetan Buddhism practised in Tibet, Mongolia, Bhutan and parts of Nepal and North India (Chapter 4). All these schools of

Buddhism are also nowadays present in Europe, North America and Australia, and to a lesser extent in South America and Africa (see Map 2). A quick Internet search reveals that the estimated number of Buddhists worldwide varies hugely: from about 350 million[1] for the most conservative to 1.6 billion[2] for the most sanguine. The CIA World Factbook gives the figure of nearly 500 million in 2013.[3] However, these figures do not include Buddhists from the People's Republic of China, and from countries that do not list Buddhism as a separate category but as part of 'other' religious affiliation, and therefore certainly underestimate the actual number.

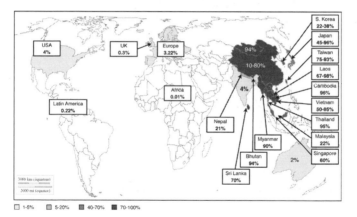

1-5%   5-20%   40-70%   70-100%

▲ Figure 0.2 Map 2: Buddhists in the world

Ning, Haruki, Jin Yen, and Robert's religious practices may not be the same, but their similarities are found in most contemporary and historical manifestations of Buddhism. They centre around three main poles: generosity, morality and contemplation. The majority of practising Buddhists in the world at the very least make regular offerings to a home shrine, a local temple, or a particular Buddhist teacher. They also seek to follow ethical rules in their daily lives and, maybe less frequently, to include a period of contemplation or meditation in their religious practice.

▲ Figure 0.3 Home shrine, Burma

▶ Buddhism's common roots

The practices and doctrines that link all the various strands of Buddhism hark back to a core of common teachings that were developed in India over the course of nearly two millennia. All Buddhist traditions consider that the historical source of these teachings is Siddhattha Gotama (Skt: Siddhārtha Gautama), a prince who left his life of abundance and pleasure to pursue the ascetic path and become a 'buddha', an awakened one. His teachings emphasized a middle path between the ascetic's austere life and his withdrawal from society, and the householder's more self-indulgent and socially enmeshed life (Chapter 1). Doctrinally, Buddhist teachings were steeped in the dominant religious milieu of ancient India, and shared its fundamental worldview and concepts, in particular that beings go through an endless cycle of rebirth and death (*saṃsāra*) that is characterized by suffering and dissatisfaction (*duḥkha/dukkha*) from which the wise seek release or liberation (*mokṣa/mokkha*).

However, in many ways, especially in its understanding of the spiritual path to obtain liberation, and of the nature of liberation itself, Buddhism differed significantly from contemporary religious traditions. It also differed socially, as it advocated a type of society based on a symbiotic arrangement in which the monastic and lay communities provided each other with the specific fruits of their lifestyle: spiritual teachings and benefits on the monastic side, and material support on the lay side (Chapter 2). This entailed adaptations and variations to local social systems, and had a profound impact on women's roles and status in the various cultures in which Buddhist teachings flourished. Full-fledged female monastic communities developed and still exist in some countries, such as Taiwan and Korea, while lay women play a crucial role as wholly involved patrons and supporters in all Buddhist societies (Chapter 3).

The Four Noble Truths are the most succinct summary of Buddhist teachings: life is suffering (*duḥkha/dukkha*) (1); it has a cause (2) and can be ended (3) by following the path that the Buddha teaches (4). These Four Noble Truths can be unpacked in the full range of Buddhist doctrines and concepts. There is a difference of emphasis between Western perception and Buddhist ideas and practices in Asian countries. While the Four Noble Truths are a fundamental teaching of Buddhism, they have been greatly emphasized in the Western approach, as opposed to more traditional Asian teachings, which usually focus on developing faith (*śraddhā/saddhā*), generosity (*dāna*) and morality (*sīla*) (Chapter 4).

The Buddhist path is undertaken over many lives as beings go through *saṃsāra*, and the realm and status in which they are reborn in each life depend on the moral quality of their actions (*karma/kamma*) in previous lives. Actions that are virtuous (*kuśala/kusala*) have pleasant results in this and future lives, and actions that are not virtuous (*akuśala/akusala*) have unpleasant results. One way Buddhists seek to obtain rebirth in better circumstances, including in the higher god realms, is by making merit (*puṇya/puñña*). Merit-making activities include all virtuous activities (such as being generous or helpful to one's neighbours), although they are more systematically institutionalized through devotional activities, such as making offerings to Buddha statues, giving financial or material support to the monastic community (*Saṅgha*) or even buying and releasing animals normally destined for human consumption (Chapter 5).

Another aspect of the Buddhist path includes meditation (*bhāvanā*). The English word meditation, which translates the Sanskrit and Pāli term *bhāvanā*, does not capture all its connotations. It could be translated as 'developing', and in this context, it is the developing of wholesome mental and spiritual states with the aim of realizing the Buddhist path that we are concerned with. As such, *bhāvanā* comprehends a very wide range of practices that may not appear 'meditative' to someone who sees meditation as sitting cross-legged in a dark, incense-filled room (Chapter 6).

The practice of *bhāvanā* also includes devotional activities and is based on a feeling of faith (*śraddhā/saddhā*). Despite what is often thought, faith is an important aspect of Buddhist practice and a precondition of starting on the path. Faith in Buddhist thought is a sentiment of trust in the Buddha and his teachings, rather than the belief in a proposition that one does not, or cannot, know directly.[4] This state of trust and confidence is developed through devotional practices, the first of which, common to all Buddhist traditions, is the taking of refuge in the Buddha, the Dharma (the Buddhist teachings) and the *Saṅgha* (the monastic community). Devotional practices, such as bowing, chanting and prostrations are common in all traditions. Beyond obtaining 'merit', making offerings is also a way to show devotion. While devotional activities are similar across traditions, their focus changes greatly depending not only on the tradition being practised, but often on individual practitioners themselves (Chapter 7).

Buddhism's experiential and analytical approach to describing reality and human experience is one of the aspects that have attracted many Westerners. Reality and human experience are analysed down to their smallest, irreducible constituents (*dharma/dhamma*), which are like the basic building blocks of reality. The Buddhist philosophical schools that arose in India focused mainly on the nature of these *dharmas/dhammas*, and their relationship, fiercely debating among them. The Madhyamaka, for example, argued for the emptiness (*śūnyatā*) of all phenomena, and the Yogacāra contended that the non-conceptual flow of experience truly exists. These debates were taken up further in Tibetan and Chinese developments and have influenced the evolution of the Chinese and Japanese schools (Chapter 8).

The expansion of Buddhism, which started southwards and continued to North and East Asia in the early centuries of the Christian era, became globalized in the 19th and 20th centuries, when Asian immigrants settled in North America, and Westerners became interested in Buddhism and travelled to Asia to study it, bringing back teachers, teachings and texts. With the new millennium, a truly global Buddhist movement is bringing together Buddhists from all schools and regions very often around specific issues, such as the full ordination of women. As Buddhism moves into the 21st century, it encounters new challenges and opportunities (Chapter 9).

Celebrating
the Buddha

▶ A day in the life of a Thai Theravāda Buddhist

Vesak (its Singhalese name) is the day which celebrates the birth, awakening and death of the Buddha. It falls on the full moon of the sixth lunar month (usually May in the solar calendar), and is celebrated throughout the Buddhist world in different ways. In Thailand, Vesak is called Visakha Puja Day and is an opportunity to make merit that few Thai Buddhists miss. This Vesak, as usual, Ning is going to the local *wat*, the temple. For the occasion, she is wearing a white blouse, with a *paa-tung*, a traditional Thai silk *sarong* worn by women. In Thailand, it is customary to go to the temple dressed more formally and traditionally than on ordinary days, just as it was expected to wear Sunday clothes to attend church in Christian countries in the past. The colour white is often worn by lay people on such occasions, because it is associated with a liminal state, just as novices and lay people on retreats wear white to mark off their special status: not fully ordained, but no longer fully in the world. The special colour symbolizes commitment to the lay precepts (see 100 Ideas section), which one seeks to uphold more rigorously.

The *wat* is more crowded than usual because people are eager to make merit on this special day, and Ning has to squeeze her way to find a space to sit in the *vihāra*, the building that holds the main Buddha image on the temple grounds. As she sits down on the floor, her feet respectfully tucked under her, she bows down three times to the seated

Buddha image at the front of the *vihāra*: to the Dhamma, the Buddha's teachings, and the *Saṅgha*, the monastic community represented by the monks and abbot who sit below the Buddha facing the assembly.

The abbot is paying homage to the Buddha with the Pāli declaration 'Homage to the Blessed One, the Arahant, the Fully Awakened One'. People around her are holding their hands in prayer, with their head slightly bowed. The homage to the Buddha is followed by the recitation of the five precepts by all those present. Everyone has in front of them an ornate silver-coloured metal bowl in which they have arranged their offerings. After the taking of the five precepts, a white thread (*sai sinn*) is unrolled and passed to each monk and members of the audience to hold as a material symbol of spiritual power. The abbot and the monks then chant a *sutta*, a sacred text from the Pāli canon.

At the end of the *sutta*, people get up, carrying their bowls, to line up outside the *vihāra* to give their offerings. As they walk by a table on which begging bowls are set, they add to them, taking from their own bowl the offerings which they have brought (fruit, packets of cooked rice, snacks, drinks, flowers and incense) which all will be distributed to the monks. In the meantime, in the *vihāra*, home-cooked dishes are being placed on a mat in front of the monks.

When everyone is back from making offerings, the abbot again gives a short homage to the Buddha, before he and the other monks are served from the dishes placed in front of them. First paying homage to the Buddha, the abbot gives a Dhamma talk, in which he explains how to lead a virtuous life according to the Buddhist doctrine, relating it to everyday life. At the end of the sermon, Ning pours water from a pitcher that she has brought for this purpose into her now empty bowl, as the abbot recites a blessing dedicating the merit of their activities for the welfare and happiness of all beings. For those not pouring water, it is enough to hold onto the person doing so to share in the merit. It is believed that the pouring of water seals the transfer of merit to all beings, and therefore represents a truly generous (and therefore meritorious) action, as the merit accrued from giving alms to the monks, and listening to the Dharma, is not selfishly kept to oneself. Thais also include their deceased loved ones and relatives in this transfer of merit.

On holy days, Theravāda Buddhists seek to undertake an activity in each of the three aspects of the path (see Chapter 4): good conduct (sīla) including generosity (dāna), meditation (bhāvanā), and wisdom (prajñā/paññā). With the offerings to the monks, and the taking of the five precepts, Ning has fulfilled good conduct, with the listening of the suttas, and of the Dhamma talk, she has sought to develop wisdom. While most people will go home after the pouring of water, Ning, as one of the most devoted, remains in the vihāra, listening to the monks chanting suttas on the life of the Buddha, and meditating, thereby practising meditation. Later, a lot of people come back, and join those who have stayed, like Ning, to follow the monks in circumambulating the vihāra three times, holding candles in homage to the three Buddhist jewels: the Buddha, Dharma, and Saṅgha.

▶ Vesak Day recognized as an International Buddhist Day

In December 1999, following a request that originated at the 1998 International Buddhist Conference in Sri Lanka, the United Nations passed a resolution[5] to recognize the day of Vesak officially as an international day sacred to Buddhists at United Nations Headquarters, national offices and permanent missions. The document acknowledges the place of Buddhism as a world religion and the role of its founder, and brings together at the international level a diverse range of celebratory activities that Buddhists engage in to celebrate the birth, awakening and death of the Buddha. Interestingly, the document by giving the date of the Buddha's birth as 623 BCE also raises a question that has occupied scholars for a long time: what can be confidently said about the historical Buddha?

▶ The historical Buddha: did the Buddha really exist?

Dates for the Buddha vary greatly between traditions, from the very early dates such as 949 BCE, found in the Eastern tradition, to the latest date, 623 BCE, adopted in the Southern tradition, and endorsed by the UN document. The scholarly consensus is now for a later date of around 400 BCE for the Buddha's death, placing his life and teachings in the 5th century BCE.[6] While we can find corroborating evidence for the historical Jesus or Muhammad in sources outside the respective traditions, our knowledge about the Buddha's life is found uniquely in the Buddhist scriptures, and this has led some to question the historicity of the Buddha. However, despite the lack of historical evidence for the life of the Buddha, it is widely accepted that there was such a person, around the 5th century BCE in Northern India, who founded the school of thought that has become the world religion known as Buddhism.

Connections

The term 'buddha' is not a name, it is a title meaning the 'awakened one', the 'enlightened one'. In the scriptures, the Buddha is also referred to as the Bhagavat (the 'Blessed One'), and the Tathāgata (the 'One Thus-Gone'). As such the historical Buddha is not unique, and all Buddhist traditions have lists of successive Buddhas. Many Buddhist traditions are awaiting the future Buddha, the Bodhisattva Maitreya (Pāli: Bodhisatta Metteya). In the traditions of the Mahāyāna, there are countless Buddhas and Bodhisattvas (beings on the path to awakening) said to exist in different realms.

▶ The life of the Buddha

The Buddha's story is often presented as a biography, but it is more meaningful to understand it as an archetype, which applies to all Buddhas in all ages.[7] This is certainly how Buddhist traditions understand it: while the Tibetan tradition organizes the Buddha's life story in 12 Great Acts, in the Pāli texts of Theravāda Buddhism, there are as many as 30 deeds or traits that all Buddhas must perform or possess as the rule.[8] But the life story of the Buddha can further be understood as the embodiment of the Buddhist path, illustrating in a persuasive narrative, the very truth that the Buddha taught: that of the Middle Way between the indulgences and luxuries of a prince's life and the austerities and privations of an ascetic;[9] a story that has captivated imaginations from the bas-reliefs of the monastic complexes of Amaravāti and Nāgārjunikoṇḍa in 2nd century Northern India to 20th century comic strips and films featuring Hollywood stars, and including novels by Nobel prize winners such as Hermann Hesse's *Siddhartha*.

However, while the story of the Buddha is clearly set in a specific time and place, its main themes – existential anguish, human finitude, the quest for meaning and transcendence, rejection of the world, and eventually resolution – resonate beyond that time and place with all those who have wondered about the purpose and meaning of life. It is striking that the majority of Buddhist converts in Western countries in the second half of the 20th century are from middle-class and upper-middle-class backgrounds.[10] People living in the midst of abundance readily identify with a 5th-century BCE Indian prince who, despite a life of hedonistic pleasures, came to the realization that suffering is an unavoidable aspect of life, whatever one's personal background and circumstances.

The status of the Buddha: is the Buddha a god or a man?

It is often emphasized that the Buddha was merely a man who achieved spiritual awakening, yet when one examines the account of his life, the main aspects of which are found in all traditions, many elements seem more characteristic of a god than of a human being. While the Lokottaravāda (supramundane) tradition saw the Buddha's terrestrial life as a 'show' played out of compassion for all sentient beings, in which the Buddha only *appeared* to be ordinary, it is fair to say that most traditions see the Buddha as a real human being who has achieved an extraordinary (but still human) state. In the same way that it is Christ's humanity that makes his sacrifice redemptory, it is the Buddha's humanity that makes his path accessible to all human beings.

Beyond certain aspects of his life story, the question about the nature of the Buddha is also linked to the way he is regarded in Buddhist cultures. In Thailand, Buddha images are covered in gold leaf and offered flowers, incense, candles, and monastic robes. They are treated with respect; as seen in the description of Ning's attendance at a Visakha Puja Day, homage and praise to the Buddha are given repeatedly during celebrations. Monks and lay people alike bow with respect to the Buddha image in the *vihāra*. For Westerners who came into contact with Buddhist cultures, this amounted to idolatry. However,

▲ Figure 1.1 Buddha image covered in gold leaf, Thailand

Buddhist images are not idols. At a basic level, especially in the Theravāda tradition, they are reminders of the Buddha and the qualities he had to perfect to become the awakened one. At another level, through consecration rituals, and for most Buddhist traditions, including the Theravāda, they come to partake of the power and spirit of the being they represent.[11] A useful metaphor may be that of a candle lit from an ever-burning fire: the candle is a reminder of the fire and partakes of its qualities.

▶ Is Buddhism a religion?

This discussion about the status of the Buddha extends to the nature of Buddhism itself. Many have claimed that it is more a philosophy of life than a religion, or a science of the mind. There is no unanimity about the definition of religion but, broadly speaking, the only definition of religion that would possibly exclude Buddhism is one that postulates belief in an omniscient, omnipotent, creator god. (This would of course exclude other traditions that do not posit such a being.) If we accept that religions share a set of characteristics that may include, but is not *limited* to, a concern with the afterlife, a moral code, a cosmology, institutions, doctrines, rituals and practices, then all Buddhist traditions are decidedly religious.

The interesting question therefore is not so much whether Buddhism is a religion (most if not all Buddhists in Asia would certainly and emphatically say it is, and so would scholars), but why, in the minds of many Westerners, Buddhism has acquired this reputation of not being one. I suggest that there are two aspects to this perception. The first, and by far the more significant, is rooted in a rejection of institutionalized Christianity that arose during the Enlightenment and developed into a full-blown rejection of religion. This is the attitude that is still found today in people who claim that they are spiritual but not religious. The second aspect is in part related to the history of the Western encounter of Buddhism, which first occurred in the colonial context. Put succinctly, many Buddhist leaders in Asia feel the need to present Buddhism as a 'rational' philosophy that fits within a scientific worldview. For example, a canonical text like the *Kālāma Sutta* is repeatedly referred to as presenting a dominant Buddhist approach of rational enquiry, or emphasis is put on the Abhidharma (Pāli: Abhidhamma) as a science of the mind that preceded Western psychology by thousands of years.

To close this brief discussion, it may be useful to remember that the Buddha, as portrayed in the canonical texts, did not present his teachings as a philosophy or a psychology, but as the path to the end of suffering and the end of rebirth in *saṃsāra*. He presented them as a way to understand the ultimate truth and attain the ultimate reality.

▶ Historical highlights: the arrival of Buddhism in Southeast Asia

Theravāda Buddhism is predominantly practised in Sri Lanka and continental Southeast Asia (Cambodia, Laos, Myanmar (also known as Burma) and Thailand). Theravāda is characterized by a sacred text, the Pāli canon; ordination lineages, which the tradition links back directly to the Buddha; and an orthodox interpretative framework focused on the works of Buddhaghosa, a 5th-century Singhalese monk. Theravādins (those who practise Theravāda Buddhism) consider their tradition to be closer to what the original teachings and practices might have been at the time of the Buddha. Despite scholarly consensus that some texts of the Pāli canon represent one of the earliest layers of Buddhism, it must be recognized that Theravāda Buddhism is a product of historical and social processes, and therefore is as authentic as, but no more than, other forms of Buddhism.

According to the tradition, Aśoka (r. 269-232 BCE), the first Indian emperor, is said to have promoted Buddhism officially, and sent his son, Mahinda, and his daughter, Saṅghamittā, to Sri Lanka. Another mission was allegedly sent to Southeast Asia around the same time (although this is not supported by archaeological evidence). It is worth keeping in mind that Southeast Asia went through an extensive process of Indianization between the 2nd century BCE and the 9th century CE: local populations incorporated, and were transformed by, Indian social, cultural and religious ideas and values, giving the region a largely unified worldview, in which Buddhist sects and Brahmanical cults spread. Chinese pilgrims from the 5th and 7th centuries report that, indeed, many different Buddhist sects flourished in Sri Lanka and Southeast Asia at the time. In Sri Lanka, Theravāda Buddhism was established as the sole sect in 1165. In Southeast Asia, Theravāda Buddhism provided a unifying focus for bringing together disparate political entities.

By the 14th century, most of the area that now comprises Cambodia, Laos, Myanmar and Thailand was predominantly Theravāda Buddhist. The Theravāda common identity was forged through centuries of exchange between the religious centres in Sri Lanka and those in the regions that are now Burma, Cambodia, Laos and Thailand, and this close relationship within the South and Southeast Asian Theravāda community continues today, and can be seen as far afield as the United States, where it is not unusual to see a Thai temple serving mostly a Lao population with Sri Lankan, Thai, Lao and Western monks.

Monasticism
and society

▶ A day in the life of a Japanese monk

Haruki is fast asleep when the wake-up bell is vigorously rung by a fellow monk running down the corridor that lines the *sōdō*, the monks' hall in the Zen monastery, as he does every morning at 4.30 a.m. Haruki quickly puts on his black robe, and files along with his fellow monks to the wash room where they carefully wash their faces and heads in a prescribed manner. The washroom, toilets and monks' hall are three buildings called the 'silent places' in which monks are not allowed to speak. Haruki returns to the *sōdō* and sits, facing the wooden wall, on a cushion placed on a *tatami* on the elevated platform that surrounds the hall. Now is the time for morning *zazen*, a period of silent meditation that is the core of Sōtō Zen Buddhism. A senior monk, holding the *kyōsaku* (a flat wooden stick), is slowly walking behind the training monks, sometimes striking them ritually across the shoulders to encourage or rouse them from their drowsiness.

Another bell is struck indicating the end of the morning *zazen*, Haruki and the other training monks walk to the *hatto* (Dharma Hall) to attend the morning service during which *sūtras* are chanted. At the end of the service, another bell rings: it is time for the morning meal, which traditionally consists of rice soup and pickled vegetables, and is taken in the monks' hall where the monks sit on their cushions, chanting, holding their hands at face level, palms together, while they wait to receive the food from the monastery kitchen. As with every daily activity, every gesture during the meal is ritualized and carefully structured: the serving monk places the rice pot on a small stool in front of each monk, who holds his bowl with both hands. When he has finished serving, the receiving monk gestures his thanks, places the bowl in front of him, raises his hand to face level, palms together, and bows. The serving monk also bows before picking up the stool and the rice pot again. Before eating, the monks raise their bowls to their heads, and at the end of the meal, they rinse them with hot water and wipe them dry.

Breakfast is followed by a period of work, which can include labour in the garden or kitchen, or cleaning the monastery. Today, Haruki is cleaning the long wooden-floor corridors that link the seven buildings that form a traditional Zen monastery. Pressing a cloth with their palms, and bending over, Haruki and several other monks quickly run the length of the corridors to the sound of the big 'work drum' that is rhythmically struck while the training monks are working. This is also the only time that monks can run. At noon, Haruki joins the other monks in the *butsuden*, the Buddha Hall, for the noon service, during which they chant *sūtras*. The afternoon follows a similar pattern with *zazen* interspersed with work. At night, they all sit in another session of *zazen*, before the night bell announces the time to lie down on the tatami on which they sleep. It is 9 p.m., and Haruki's day has ended.[12]

◗ Becoming a Buddhist monk or nun

At the time of the Buddha, according to the canonical texts, monks were ordained with the simple words 'come monk'. Nowadays, the ordination procedure is more complex and lengthy. There is a minimum age required to take full ordination, although children as young as 6 or 7 could traditionally (and, in some traditions, still do – see the photo opposite) become novices in a monastery, often to gain an education that they would not otherwise be able to receive. The reasons for ordination are diverse, but many become ordained today to 'live the spiritual life for the complete ending of suffering' as they were said to do at the time of the Buddha. In an anthropological study of *mae chis* (Thai female renouncers – see Chapter 3), Monica Lindberg Falk points out that the *mae chis'* main reason for leaving the lay life is deeply anchored in their interest and faith in the Buddhist path, and is expressed in doctrinal terms by the First and Third Noble Truths taught by the Buddha (Chapter 4): they have realized the nature of existence as suffering and want to find release from suffering.[13] In many cases, this would be the main reason for ordaining as a monk or nun, as the monastic life is still thought to be the best way to advance to the Buddhist goal of awakening. In some cases, as the status of the monk is highly respected in Buddhist societies, some may choose ordination partly to improve their social status.

▲ Figure 2.1 Tibetan novices waiting to greet the Karmapa, Bodhgayā, India

▶ The monastic community's development

According to the Pāli canon, after the Buddha delivered his first sermon to the five renouncers with whom he had practised severe austerities before becoming the Buddha, he encountered Yasa, a layman, and taught him the Dhamma, and gave him and his 54 companions ordination by instructing them 'come, monks' thereby establishing the *Saṅgha*, the Buddhist monastic community. Most Buddhist monastic traditions trace their origins to that episode. As the community grew and became more established, rules became necessary. They were preserved in the *Vinaya*, the monastic code of conduct, which describes each rule and the occasion that prompted the rule to be established.

The *Vinaya* rules structure monastic life and interactions with the lay community. In addition, the extreme detail of some of the rules on deportment (for example, how to hold one's arms when walking, or how one eats – sticking one's tongue out, chomping, or making sucking noises are among minor offences) seems to indicate that the *Vinaya* also serves as a mental training tool for monks and nuns, as it requires them to be constantly and rigorously mindful of their behaviour.

Connections

Despite the development of many different *Vinayas* (18 schools, each with their own *Vinaya*, are recorded in the traditional accounts) only three are now used: monks in Sri Lanka and Southeast Asia follow the Pāli Theravāda *Vinaya*; in China, Korea and Japan, monks and nuns follow the Dharmaguptaka *Vinaya* translated into Chinese in the 5th century; and in Tibet and Mongolia, it is the *Vinaya* of the Mūlasarvāstivāda, translated into Tibetan in the 9th century, that is followed. Despite some differences in the rules of the extant *Vinayas*, they share the same structure and essential content.

▶ The monastic code of conduct (*Vinaya*)

A large section of the *Vinaya* deals with interactions between the monks and nuns and the lay community, addressing issues such as proper behaviour when begging for alms in villages, and teaching lay people. This underlines the highly interdependent relationship that exists between the *Saṅgha* and laity. From the beginning, monks and nuns were intended to interact with lay people on a daily basis as many *Vinaya* rules prevent them from being self-sufficient. For example, in Classical Buddhism, and still in Theravāda Buddhism, they cannot work, or grow or cook food, or store cooked food in their quarters, and therefore must rely on the generosity of lay donors for their subsistence.

At the doctrinal level, the interdependence between the laity and the *Saṅgha* rests on a subtle exchange: the laity provides the means of subsistence to the monastic community in the form of food, lodgings, clothes and other necessities. Obviously, they also provide new members to the monastic community. In return, the *Saṅgha* serves as a field of merit, that is, by receiving alms from lay people, they allow them to perform a virtuous action. While the *Saṅgha* as a whole is a field of merit, individual monks or nuns can be considered greater or lesser fields of merit according to the perceived quality of their conduct and spiritual practice, that is, it is believed that the good consequences of giving to these particular monks or nuns are greater. In Theravāda Buddhism, the Buddha is considered to be the greatest field of merit. Practically, in all traditions, the *Saṅgha* also performs a variety of rituals on behalf of lay people.

Connections

In the *Vinaya*, monks are not allowed to touch women, or to be alone in an enclosed space with a woman. As a result, a monk will not shake a woman's hand, nor sit next to one, and will accept items handed to him by a woman only when first placed on a surface from which he can pick it up. The main intention of these restrictions is to avoid temptation that could arise from close proximity with a woman (in a traditionally heterosexual context) and to avoid situations that could be misconstrued by others and result in monks being charged with punishable offences.

▶ Buddhism and politics

The interaction between the *Saṅgha* and the lay community has also always involved interaction with the ruling classes. The Buddha of the canonical texts is shown with many rulers of his time. Some texts even propose a concept of the ideal ruler, the 'wheel-turning' monarch (*cakravartin/cakkavatti*) who rules according to the Dharma (Pāli: Dhamma) and possesses ten royal virtues.

The ideal of the *dhammarāja*, the exemplary Buddhist king, has remained strongly evocative, especially in Southeast Asia. For example, in Thailand it was called upon to reinforce King Bhumidol's stature following his accession to the throne in 1946. Since the great Mauryan Emperor Aśoka whom the tradition has revered as the historical embodiment of this ideal, Buddhism has been used by aspiring or established political powers as a unifying force to bring together sometimes ethnically and culturally disparate populations, such as in the regions that are now Burma and Thailand. Buddhism was also perceived to bring a civilizing influence in countries like 6th century Japan and 8th century Tibet.

Ruling authorities in Asia have also relied on Buddhist ideas and practices as a legitimizing strategy. For example, in 7th century China, the Empress Wu Zetian's accession to the throne was justified with the claim that she was an incarnation of the future Buddha Maitreya. A more recent example is that of the Burmese military *junta* who, after years of marginalizing the Burmese *Saṅgha*, engaged in vast merit-making activities, including the construction of temples in Rangoon and Mandalay in the 1980s. Claiming Buddhist ideals to further secular aims is not restricted to ruling authorities, and many groups have fought established governments on the basis of Buddhist principles. In 15th-century Japan, Pure Land followers regularly revolted against the authorities, sometimes in great numbers. Since the 20th century, Tibetan Buddhists have struggled to retain their religion and culture under Chinese Communist rule.

Buddhist beliefs and values can be harnessed for numerous political goals, and recent events in Asia have challenged the Western image of Buddhism as a peaceful and tolerant religion. Over the last two decades, Nationalist movements in Sri Lanka, Thailand and Burma (Myanmar) have turned Buddhism into a nationalist device that serves to separate the 'true' citizens from others with monks clamouring for the purity of the nation and religion. Burma in particular has been at the forefront of the news in recent months and, at the time of writing (June 2013), Buddhist monks' speeches have sparked anti-Muslim riots and bloodshed in which more than 200 Muslims have been killed, and 150,000 displaced.[14] The violence threatens to shatter the fragile stability that followed the devolution of power from the military *junta* to a democratically elected government since 2010.[15]

▲ Figure 2.2 Burma Rally, London

▶ Historical highlights: the arrival of Buddhism in Japan

According to the *Japanese Chronicles (Nihonshoki)*,[16] Buddhism came to Japan in the 6th century *ce*, when the king of the Korean kingdom of Paekche sent an image of Śākyamuni Buddha, *sūtra* scrolls and banners to the Japanese emperor Kimmei. The account in the *Nihonshoki* points to a political struggle between the two major clans that was resolved decades later in the accession to power of the Soga clan with Empress Suiko and Prince Regent Shotōku, a committed Buddhist who is said to have written commentaries on three Mahāyāna sutras, and used Buddhism as a unifying influence in a Japan divided into competing clans. Under his aegis, the first national Buddhist temple was built at Nara in 607 *ce*. The strong relationship that was thereby instituted between the imperial house and Buddhism was further strengthened in the 8th century with the establishment of the Japanese capital at Nara. The state strongly promoted Buddhism, building magnificent temples, such as Nara's Tōdai-ji temple, financially supporting monks and temples, and encouraging the growth of Buddhism by promoting exchanges of clergy, texts and artefacts with China.[17]

The two sects established in the 9th century, the Tiantai of Saichō (767-822) and the Shingon of Kūkai (774-835), are still part of Japanese Buddhism today: the Tiantai whose main monastery Enryaku-ji was extremely influential until the 15th century, has branched out in many of the Pure Land sects, and retains a steady following; the Shingon sect thrives with over 12,000 temples and 12 million followers.

As Buddhism expanded to the common people, both the Shingon and Tiantai schools recognized the *kamis* (divine beings of Shinto) as manifestations of Buddhas and Bodhisattvas, thereby integrating them into Buddhist cosmology.

The new teachings of the Pure Land emerged in the 10th century, in a climate of political turmoil and natural disasters, probably as a reaction to the apocalyptic idea that *mappō* (Chinese: *mofa*), a time of chaos and affliction accompanied by the decline of the Buddhist teachings, had come. The Tiantai monk Hōnen (1133–1212) is seen as the founder of the Pure Land sect (*Jodōshu* or *Jōdo-shin-shū*); he travelled through the countryside, preaching widely to the people, and advocating the *nembutsu*, the recitation of Buddha Amitābha's name (Japanese: Amida) to obtain rebirth in his Western Pure Land. A follower of Hōnen, Shinran (1173–1262) rejected celibacy, and paved the path for a married clergy, which became hereditary.

Three more major schools of Japanese Buddhism developed in the 13th century. Eisai (1141–1215) introduced Rinzai Zen which, with its focus on discipline, became a favourite of the samurais. A student of Eisai, and Tiantai monk, Dōgen (1200–53) returned from studying in China, and advocated *zazen*, sitting meditation, and a rigorous and simple monastic life, founding the Sōtō Zen school (in which Haruki above is ordained). Finally, another Tiantai monk, Nichiren (1222–82) wished to recognize the main text of the Tiantai school, the *Lotus Sūtra*, and rejected all forms of spiritual practice, except for devotion to the *Lotus Sūtra*. His followers became the Nichiren school. These three schools are still extant in modern-day Japan, and also spread to North America and Europe in the 20th century.

In the 21st century, traditional Buddhism in Japan is facing a serious decline, with the numbers of countryside temples, and membership at remaining temples, steadily decreasing.[18] However, this decline may be counterbalanced by the growth of new religious movements in Japan, many of them inspired by Buddhism, and not all of them as controversial as the Soka Gakkai, an organization that has successfully spread outside Japan in recent decades, or the infamous Aum Shinrikyo, the cult responsible for the sarin gas attack in Tokyo's underground in 1995.

Women
and Buddhism

A day in the life of a Taiwanese Buddhist nun

Jin Yen wakes up at 5 a.m. to do her devotional practice. She has a quick breakfast, and as it is just after 6 a.m., she has time to do some reading for her classes. Jin Yen is 48 and she has been a nun for 22 years. She usually lives in a monastery in the North of Taiwan, but she has been sent by the abbess of the monastery to study for a PhD in a British university. Dedicated and promising nuns and monks are sometimes sent to pursue academic degrees in European and North American universities. When they come back they can share their learning with their fellow nuns and monks, and with the lay people who come to night classes at the monastery. Today, she is attending a Sanskrit class, so she prepares some food to take to university, as it can be difficult to eat out with the dietary rules of the Bodhisattva vows she must follow, including not eating any meat, fish or eggs, nor any onion or garlic. The students in her class greet her with respect. They have become accustomed to her shaven head and grey monastic robes, and some of them have even decided to attend the weekly meditation class she leads at the university chaplaincy. While her life on a British campus is different from the life she leads at the monastery, she tries to keep a similar routine, alternating between periods of meditation and chanting, and periods of study, teaching and work. This afternoon, she is participating in a meeting to organize activities to raise funds for the victims of the Tōhoku earthquake in Japan (11 March 2011), which killed more than 15,000 people and caused serious nuclear accidents. After that, she goes home to do a moving meditation – a very slow type of yoga, before she heads out again to the meditation class. Her day ends at 9.30 p.m. with another 15-minute meditation and prayer session in front of the Buddha on her desk.

▶ Women in historical Buddhism

Before we start examining 'women' in any religious tradition, or human phenomenon for that matter, it is important to clarify why such an examination is necessary. Women obviously represent half of humankind. However, it is widely acknowledged that in most, if not all, societies, their voices, experiences and activities are not represented proportionately to their actual presence and are, in many cases, marginalized or entirely ignored. Religious traditions often subsume women's experience within a generic male that allegedly includes women. However, the generic male automatically excludes women. For example, when the Buddhist texts tell us that the Buddha refused to ordain women several times before finally accepting, it reveals that the spiritual path of women is not expected to be the same as that of men. Therefore, women need special attention if we are to paint a realistic and comprehensive picture of historical and contemporary Buddhism, lest we ignore half of it.

Scholarly research on the attitudes found in the canonical texts reveal two main strands: on the one hand, women's ability to reach awakening is clearly and unequivocally stated, and gender is irrelevant to attaining the goal; on the other, a few texts are virulently misogynistic. In the Pāli canon, the misogynistic passages are very few, but close examination shows a very subtle bias against women; for example, their spiritual achievements are always lower than those of men in a spiritual hierarchy with laywomen at the bottom and monks at the top. Another subtle bias is that the most prominent women, especially those closest to the Buddha, are laywomen. While women of all social ranks are depicted interacting with the Buddha, no individual nun is, and women are mostly shown as daughters, wives and mothers. This allows us to conclude that, by and large, Buddhist texts are, by modern standards, generally conservative when it comes to women and gender roles.

However, it may be useful to consider that these texts were produced in socio-cultural environments that were vastly different from those in which we live today and that, by emphasizing women's socially acceptable roles within the Buddhist context, Buddhist texts were opening up the Buddhist path to women who may not have had access to it otherwise. Furthermore, it is also noteworthy that Buddhist canonical texts have preserved texts, such as the *Therīgāthā*, authored by women who had attained awakening, and *suttas* in which eloquent nuns are shown teaching the Dhamma. When these are considered in their socio-historical context, it becomes possible to appreciate that they were comparatively very progressive.

▶ Nuns in canonical and historical Buddhism

The description of the foundation of the nuns' order has drawn a lot of attention, especially as it underlines the ambivalence about women found in Buddhist texts. In the Pāli account, Mahāpajāpatī, the Buddha's maternal aunt and stepmother, asks the Buddha to allow women to be ordained. The Buddha initially refuses, and Mahāpajāpatī leaves dejected. Some time later, joined by 500 women from the Buddha's clan, she reiterates her plea, which is met, again, by the Buddha's refusal. As she leaves the Buddha's residence, she comes across the Buddha's attendant, Ānanda, who expresses concern. She explains what has occurred and Ānanda immediately takes it upon himself to convince the Buddha to allow women to be ordained. However, the Buddha is not so easily persuaded, and Ānanda has to repeat his request twice. The second time, he changes his approach and asks the Buddha whether women, if allowed to ordain, would be able to reach awakening. The Buddha acknowledges that they would, which prompts Ānanda to follow up by asking him again to grant Mahāpajāpatī her request. The Buddha finally consents, but institutes eight rules that Mahāpajāpatī must accept for all women who will seek ordination. These rules in effect put nuns under the institutional authority of monks.

The Buddha's initial refusals and subsequent institution of the eight rules have been considered a telling illustration of Buddhism's ambivalence towards women. Nonetheless, it is noteworthy that the order of nuns was established and flourished until the 12th century, when the last inscriptions mentioning nuns are found in India, and was transmitted to Sri Lanka and East Asia. It is unclear why the order of nuns died out in India before Buddhism itself disappeared, but some scholars have argued that the eight rules might have played a role by insinuating that nuns were not as worthy of offerings as monks, and therefore were not as supported as monks by the laity leaving them in precarious conditions, and eventually leading to their disappearance.[19]

The order of nuns was transmitted throughout Asia in different ways. The Theravāda tradition holds that Emperor Aśoka sent his daughter Saṅghamittā to Sri Lanka to establish the order of nuns there. Following the Tamil invasion of 1050, the Singhalese *Saṅgha* was destroyed, and while the monks' order was re-established with the help of Burmese monks in 1070, the nuns' order was not re-established in Sri Lanka until 1998 (see Chapter 9). In Southeast Asia, the nuns' order was only established in Burma, but disappeared after the 13th-century invasion of the Burmese capital by the Mongols.[20]

▶ Buddhist nuns today

With the disappearance of the Indian, Singhalese and Burmese orders, the Theravāda lineage of fully ordained nuns died out. Orders of monastic women, holding eight or ten precepts, evolved in Sri Lanka and Southeast Asia, and are still extant today, but they are not recognized

▲ Figure 3.1 East Asian nuns chanting at Mahābodhi Temple, Bodhgayā, India

as part of the Buddhist monastic community, and do not benefit from the same advantages and opportunities as the monks.

In East and Northern Asia, only China and Korea have had an order of fully ordained nuns. In Tibet, the nuns' order never became firmly established, and there are only novice nuns. Japanese nuns are not ordained according to any Vinaya lineage, but in a way specific to the mainstream Japanese schools that emerged from the Tiantai and according to which they follow the Bodhisattva precepts.

A global movement has been seeking to re-establish the ordination lineages for women in the Theravāda and Tibetan traditions over the last two decades (see Chapter 9). Beyond the importance of offering women access to the religious path of their choice, the re-establishment of the women's order is also valuable for the laity, especially laywomen, who greatly benefit from having access to fully ordained nuns and female monasteries. Women feel inspired by such nuns, and also feel that they can establish a closer and more fruitful relationship with nuns than with monks. They are more comfortable speaking with them about family, personal or specifically feminine issues than they are with monks. Clearly, the lack of such nuns impacts negatively on Buddhist women's spiritual lives.[21]

▶ Buddhist women around the world

Not all Buddhist women wish to ordain as nuns, and many express their spirituality through lay practice. As we have seen, in the canonical texts, women are often described as fulfilling their spiritual paths through their social roles of daughters, wives and mothers. This is still true today, and many women seek to integrate Buddhist values within their daily lives, usually in inconspicuous ways, whether in traditional Buddhist societies or new environments. In Asia, as well as in Europe and North America, lay Buddhist women have been involved in a variety of endeavours that draw on Buddhist values and ideals. For example, the largest share of the support provided to monastic institutions and temples, such as food preparation, and building and ground maintenance, is usually done by laywomen. In Taiwan, for example, laywomen donate an extraordinary amount of time to cooking for special occasions at monasteries, often waking up at 3 or 4 a.m.

to prepare food for the monks and nuns. It has been argued that women who fulfil their spiritual aspiration in these ways stay within traditionally 'female' roles, possibly implying that their contribution is somehow less valuable for it. However, it seems that this is in itself an attitude that ranks traditionally female roles as less valuable than traditionally male roles, and it is important to realize that a spiritual life can be lived fruitfully whether as a nun or as a laywoman.

▲ Figure 3.2 Laywomen sweeping temple ground, Burma

Khun Mae Siri Krinchai, Thailand[22]

Siri Krinchai (1917–2011) started insight (*vipassanā*) meditation training courses in her house in Nakhorn Ratchasima, Thailand, in the mid-1950s. Despite these humble beginnings, she gained a wide following and trained meditation teachers who use her approach to conduct meditation workshops with a wide range of students, including children, across Thailand. She is particularly well known for developing a structured one-week meditation course that is used effectively for groups of adults and children, because it involves simple steps and alternate sitting and walking meditation. The meditation sessions are interspersed with Buddhist teachings. Many of her students stress the beneficial impact of attending her meditation workshops on their personal and professional lives. Workshops based on her method are held in a variety of settings and organizations, from schools and workplaces to temples. She kept a very simple attitude throughout her life and was well respected by lay and monastic Thais, who refer to her as *Khun Mae*, 'Mother', for making the dhamma and insight meditation easily accessible to lay people. In 2002, she received the Outstanding Women in World Buddhism award for her exceptional contribution to Buddhism from an international committee of Buddhist clergy, scholars and laity on the occasion of the United Nation's International Women's Day.

Joan Halifax Roshi, USA[23]

Joan Halifax was born in New Hampshire in 1942, and spent her childhood in Georgia. She recounts that the death of her grandmother, with whom she had a close relationship, had a profound impact on her professional choices and her interest in Buddhism. She studied medical anthropology and was awarded a PhD from Tulane in 1973 before she started working with dying patients. She started studying Buddhism shortly after her grandmother's death, and her spiritual lineage draws on three different traditions of Zen

Buddhism. She studied with the Korean Master Seung Sahn for ten years, and received transmission from Thich Naht Hanh, the Vietnamese Zen Master, and Bernie Glassman, the founder of the Zen Peacemakers. Her personal style draws on these traditions, and she is known to be very direct and sometimes even confrontational, a style, she recognizes, which is not always appreciated in women. In 1992, she founded the Upaya Zen Center in Santa Fe, of which she is now the abbot and head teacher. Her Project on Being with Dying has been training professionals in end-of-life care for nearly 20 years in skills to deal with dying and death in a compassionate and skilful way. She is also the founder and director of the Upaya Prison project, which develops meditation programmes for prisoners. Her work illustrates the development of socially engaged Buddhism in North America, focusing on marginalized populations, and seeking to integrate personal practice with social action.

Venerable Chao Hwei, Taiwan

Chao Hwei was born in Burma in 1957, and moved to Taiwan when she was 10. She is maybe less well known, especially in the West, than other Taiwanese Buddhist masters, such as Dharma Master Cheng Yen who established Ciji (Buddhist Compassion Relief Tzu Chi Foundation) and she distinguishes herself with what some have seen as a radical, and sometimes controversial, approach. She is a strong advocate for human rights, women's rights and animal rights. She is willing to take controversial stances in a predominantly conservative society, as for example, when she urged the Dalai Lama to reinstate the full ordination for Tibetan nuns, and had the eight rules that subordinate nuns to monks symbolically torn up on stage at a conference in 2001, or when she celebrated a same-sex union in Taiwan in 2012.[24] Chao Hwei became a nun when she was 21, and one of the first Buddhist nuns to teach at a public school in Taiwan. She is now Professor of Religion and Director of the Research Center of Applied Ethics at Hsuan Chuang University. She is a respected scholar who has published more than 25 books on a wide range of political, social and Buddhist issues. A student of Master Shun Yin, she promotes an egalitarian approach to Buddhism. Her activism goes beyond transformation of the individual to challenge systemic inequalities in Taiwanese society, and she represents an example of Buddhist monastics who engage deeply with the social, economic and political realities of today's world.

Mindrolling Jetsün Khandro Rinpoche, India[25]

Tsering Paldrön (her birth name) was born in 1967 in the monastery founded in Kalimpong, India, by her father, Kyabje Mindrolling Trichen Gyurme Künzang Wangyal, the previous head of the Nyimgma school of Tibetan Buddhism, after he had fled Tibet. She was recognized by His Holiness the 16th Gyalwang Karmapa as the reincarnation of Khandro Ugyen Tsomo, a revered female master of the late 19th and early 20th century, and as the emanation of Yeshe Tsogyal, the consort of Padmasambhava, the mythical founder of Tibetan Buddhism (see Chapter 4). Khandro Rinpoche holds teaching lineages from the Nyimgma-pa and the Kagyu-pa Tibetan schools, and has received teachings from accomplished masters, such as Dilgo Khyentse Rinpoche, and the Dalai Lama. She also received a Western-style education in boarding schools in India, and thus possesses a broad educational background that makes her an ideal teacher in today's global context. Indeed, she started teaching widely both in Asia and in the West in 1992, and has impressed many with her demanding style.

Khandro Rinpoche is one of the very few female Tibetan teachers, but claims that gender should not be held onto as an essential characteristic of a teacher, and usually brings back gender issues to personal practice.[26] Yet, she recognizes that providing female role models, especially as a teacher, is important and, in particular, supports women's religious education with the Samten Tse Retreat Center, which she established in 1993 in India, and where Tibetan nuns can study and practise. Another defining characteristic of Khandro Rinpoche is her ecumenical approach, broadly based on the 19th century Rimé movement (Chapter 4); she brings together all four schools of Tibetan Buddhism at the Lotus Garden Retreat Centre, which she established in Virginia in 2003.

▶ Historical highlights: the arrival of Buddhism in China

While Buddhism was present in China as early as the 1st century CE when the translation and study of Buddhist texts started, it had little impact on the Chinese population until after the fall of the Han dynasty, and the invasion of the northern part of the Chinese empire by the Huns at the beginning of the 4th century ce. Until the 6th century, the northern region was ruled by non-Chinese dynasties that supported Buddhism, partly because it was not associated with the Chinese Confucian or Taoist traditions. By the 5th century, there were up to 30,000 monasteries, and over 2 million monks in that part of China. Buddhist texts brought from India through Central Asia via the Silk Road were translated and studied, especially through the impetus of Kumārajīva, a Central Asian monk who was fluent in Sanskrit and Chinese.

In the southern region, ruled by Chinese dynasties, Buddhism was perceived as a foreign 'barbarian' tradition, and did not develop as successfully as in the north. It was felt to be antithetical to many Chinese values such as the focus on family and family line, the hierarchical structure of Confucian society, and the emphasis on productive work. However, Buddhist ideas did find some receptive minds in the southern region, and by the early 5th century, there were about 2,000 monasteries there and, in the first half of the 6th century, Emperor Wu became a lay supporter of Buddhism, banning Taoism. It is also in the south that Bodhidharma, the semi-legendary founder of Chan Buddhism, is said to have arrived from India.

These two early separate regional beginnings of Buddhism in China left a mark on subsequent development after the north and south reunited under the Sui and Tang dynasties between the 6th and 10th century, with the emergence of two distinct forms of Chinese schools, some closely based on the original

Indian model, and some developing as indigenous Chinese traditions.

These early schools of Chinese Buddhism were nearly all eradicated by Emperor Wuzong (814–846), and only Chan and Pure Land survived. Chan said to have been founded by the Indian Bodhidharma, later separated into two main schools: the Linji and the Caodong schools (respectively Rinzai and Sōtō Zen in Japan – see Chapter 2). These schools differed in their conception of the path to awakening, but they both emphasized work as part of the monk's training, a notable departure from the Indian tradition.

In the following centuries, Buddhism slowly integrated with popular practices related to Taoism and Confucianism, the two indigenous traditions of China. The two schools also adopted some of each other's practices such as the recitation of the *nianfo* (see Chapter 6). By the time Mao Zedong came to power in 1949, Buddhism was still an important part of Chinese popular religious practices and remained so despite the Cultural Revolution (1966–76).

The disease and
the remedy

◗ A day in the life of an American Tibetan Buddhist

Robert lives in New York City. A few years ago, he became interested in Tibetan Buddhism, and started attending classes with Tibetan teachers. As his interest grew, he decided to convert to Buddhism formally. During the brief, simple ceremony, Robert repeated the Refuge prayer three times (see Chapter 7), before a lama cut a lock of his hair, and gave him a Dharma name, formalizing his entry into the Buddhist community.

Connections

'Lama' is the Tibetan for the Sanskrit 'guru'. The term refers to a spiritual parent or preceptor, who initiates, instructs and guides the disciple. The role of the lama/guru (who can be a lay or ordained person) is central in all Tantric traditions.

The lama also gave him a practice to perform on a daily basis, and every morning since, after he is ready for the day, Robert makes offerings to the Buddha and Bodhisattva images. He offers seven bowls of fresh water, and lights a candle, which he places between the third and fourth bowl of water. The symbolism of the water bowls is diverse. They represent material offerings of water for drinking and bathing, of flowers, incense, light, perfume and food, but also spiritual activities, such as the seven aspects of prayer described by Śantideva, the 8th century author of the *Bodhicaryāvatāra, The Way of the Bodhisattva*, a text that is still widely taught in Tibetan Buddhism. Tibetan teachers, such as the Dalai Lama, also emphasize that the main purpose of making offerings to Buddha and Bodhisattva images is to develop generosity.

This weekend, Robert is attending a teaching by His Holiness the Dalai Lama, whose topic, 'The Four Noble Truths', is one of the fundamental Buddhist doctrines. The Dalai Lama, even in the West, teaches in the traditional Tibetan style, sitting on a brocade-covered throne-like chair. He does not have a prepared lecture, and speaks during lengthy sessions, in which he addresses his theme in seemingly random fashion. However, even his jokes and his personal anecdotes highlight and illustrate the relevance of the teachings in today's world. Robert is grateful for the opportunity to attend, especially as the auditorium is filled to capacity. The crowd is very diverse and Robert can distinguish those who identify as Buddhists from the merely curious as they prostrate three times before settling down. Many Tibetans also have come to hear their exiled leader, who they see as the incarnation of compassion. Robert, inspired and moved by the Dalai Lama's palpable benevolence, returns home reflecting on the teachings he has heard during the day. As he empties the offering bowls he had set out in the morning, wipes and stacks them upside down on the altar, he determines to put these profound teachings into practice.

Connections: Tenzin Gyatso, His Holiness the 14th Dalai Lama

The Dalai Lama is a prominent figure of global Buddhism and, for many Westerners, its most popular representative. Tibetans believe beings who have attained a high level of spiritual realization can be reborn for the benefit of all beings, and can choose their place and time of rebirth. The Dalai Lama, according to this tradition, is the 14th subsequent successive reincarnation of a nephew of Tsongkhapa, the 15th century founder of the Gelug-pa school. In addition, he is also believed to be an emanation of Avalokiteśvara, the Bodhisattva of Compassion. Until 2011, the Dalai Lama was the head of the Tibetan government in exile but, contrary to what is often thought, not the leader of Tibetan Buddhism. His renown, doubtless, is due to his charisma and ability to convey and adapt the teachings of Tibetan Buddhism to a Western audience and to draw attention to the plight of the Tibetan people.

▲ Figure 4.1 Chinese one-thousand armed Avalokiteśvara with Amitābha in crown, Thailand

▶ Suffering

While the Buddha talked about 'cold and heat, hunger and thirst, contact with gnats and mosquitoes, wind and sun and snakes' in the *suttas* (S III 86), the Dalai Lama draws on his recent experience of eye surgery to illustrate the First Noble Truth according to which human life is characterized by *dukkha*, a word usually, but inadequately, translated as suffering. The term *dukkha* (Skt: *duḥkha*) points to three main inescapable aspects of life, whether we live in ancient India, or in New York City in the 21st century. First, life contains physical pain, from stubbing one's toe to much harsher pain due to illness or violence, and even the most fortunate person cannot avoid some level of physical pain. Second, life entails change, because of its impermanent nature; we change, we get ill, we grow older, and eventually we die. Even pleasant experiences are bound to change or cease: they are impermanent and cannot satisfy us forever. As a result, we are endlessly compelled to seek other pleasant experiences. The third aspect of *dukkha*, to which the Dalai Lama refers as *conditioning*, emphasizes the interrelated nature of existence: even in pleasant circumstances, such as those in which people in the modern world may find themselves – circumstances broadly comparable to the princely early life of the Buddha – the fact that suffering may affect us at any moment, or even when we are not experiencing it ourselves, that it exists in the world, is *dukkha*. The very nature of existence is *dukkha*. This does not mean that Buddhism takes a grim and depressing attitude to life, as some people claim. On the contrary, as the Dalai Lama points out in his talk, realizing and accepting the nature of life, often summarized as 'birth, sickness, ageing and death' is the starting point for the spiritual quest. This is exemplified in the story of the Buddha, who decides to give up his princely life and become a wandering ascetic after encountering the 'four sights' of an ill man, an ageing man, a corpse and an ascetic. The Dalai Lama highlights the sense of urgency that this should stir in all of us by stressing that, in Buddhist thought, human life is understood as allowing a unique opportunity for spiritual growth and reaching the ultimate goal of awakening (*nirvāṇa/nibbāna*).

Connections: the Four Noble Truths

1 The Noble Truth of Suffering: life, birth, ageing and death are suffering.

2 The Noble Truth of the Origin of Suffering: craving is the cause of suffering.

3 The Noble Truth of the Cessation of Suffering: nirvāṇa is the end of suffering.

4 The Noble Truth of the Path to the End of Suffering: the Eightfold Noble Path is the path to the end of suffering.

The origin of suffering: craving

The Pāli sutta *Setting the wheel of Dhamma in motion* (*Dhammacakkappavattana Sutta*) points to the cause of suffering as *tṛṣṇā/taṅhā*, an intense and unceasing craving that is threefold. Beings crave objects of the senses, they crave continued existence, and they crave non-existence. The canonical texts describe these cravings in a variety of ways. This phenomenon of craving, however, is not limited by time or culture and, in our modern society, it can be illustrated by our endless consumption of products and experiences: from comfort foods to exotic holidays, we are endlessly seeking to satisfy our senses. Similarly, as a society, we are obsessed with youth, and fear death to the extent that it has all but become invisible and unmentionable. Essentially, our craving for continued existence is a craving for eternal life. On the other hand, our craving for non-existence is expressed through the consumption of alcohol and drugs, which numb our sense of being alive, and ultimately culminates in high rates of addiction and even suicide.

Why does craving cause suffering? Craving often leads to attachment (upādāna): we become attached to what we crave. We want more of it; we do not want it to stop, or to disappear. We want to possess and control it. We identify with it. But attachment is incompatible with the way things are. We do not have unlimited capacity to enjoy experiences – think about the well-known physiological and psychological process of habituation: as we get used to something, it procures us less and less pleasure, and we require more and more of it in order to achieve the same effect. When we get attached to things, experiences, or people, we want them to last forever, but they do not. We ourselves do not stay the same forever. In his talk about the Four Noble Truths, the Dalai Lama points out that despite the fact that we all seek happiness and try to avoid suffering, we act and behave in ways that lead to more suffering. At the heart of this discrepancy between what we want and what really is, he argues, is a fundamental ignorance (*avidyā/avijjā*) of the way things really are: changing and impermanent.

Connections: a medical metaphor

The Buddha is often compared to a doctor who, having established a diagnosis, recommends a treatment to cure the patient. The Third Noble Truth points to the state of being cured, the cessation of suffering, which is nirvāna; the Fourth Noble Truth is the treatment, the Noble Eightfold Path. In this medical metaphor, when the disease has been entirely eradicated, the patient has attained nirvāna.

The end of suffering: nirvāṇa

The term *nirvāṇa* has become part of our everyday vocabulary in the West. It usually refers to a blissful and intensely pleasurable state. Is there some basis to this understanding of nirvāṇa? Does it mean that the Buddha is in some state of bliss and pleasure? According to the Buddhist tradition, when the Buddha sat under the Bodhi tree and attained nirvāṇa, he 'understood and penetrated' the Four Noble Truths. By seeing them, 'the root of suffering is cut, and no longer is there rebirth.' As we have seen, suffering is caused by craving and the attachment that results stems from the fundamental ignorance of the way things really are. Attaining nirvāṇa is a two-faceted event: the letting go of craving and realizing the true nature of things.[27] This should not be seen as a chronological process in which there is first ignorance and then craving, rather ignorance and craving may be better seen as the cognitive and affective facets of our being in *saṃsāra*: ignorance is our way of understanding the world, and craving our way of relating to it.

One consequence of nirvāṇa is the end of rebirth: one who has attained nirvāṇa has 'destroyed birth [and for such a one] there is no more coming to any state of being'. Two questions arise from this: what happens after one has reached awakening? And what happens after they die? Buddhism is quite clear on the first question: the Buddha is shown teaching for another 45 years after awakening, and a cursory look at other awakened beings in different Buddhist traditions, such as Milarepa in Tibetan Buddhism, shows that they also teach beings who are still mired in *saṃsāra*. But unlike those unawakened beings, the Buddha and the others who have attained nirvāṇa live free from the defilements of greed, hatred and delusion: all their actions and thoughts stem from generosity, friendliness and wisdom. On the other hand, attitudes vary regarding the second question: while the Mahāyāna teems with an abundance of Buddhas who live in Buddha realms, the Pāli texts refuse to answer it because, scholars have argued, the answer to this question is not useful for the achievement of the path that leads to the end of suffering.[28]

Connections: the Noble Eightfold Path[29]

1 Right view: seeing the Four Noble Truths

2 Right intention: desirelessness, friendliness, compassion

3 Right speech: abstaining from false, divisive and harsh speech, and from idle chatter

4 Right action: abstaining from harming life, from taking what is not given, from sexual misconduct

5 Right livelihood: not based on wrong speech and wrong action

6 Right effort: to cultivate wholesome mental states and abandon unwholesome mental states

7 Right mindfulness: contemplation of body, feeling, mind, and phenomena

8 Right concentration: practice of the four meditative states

The path to the end of suffering

The Noble Eightfold Path is the path to the cessation of suffering whose eight limbs are interdependent. They are not to be completed sequentially as, for example, a Bachelor of Art degree has to be completed before a Master's, and before a PhD, but rather they are the qualities that characterize the life of one who is on the Noble Path. Here, a distinction must be made between those who have attained a certain level of spiritual realization, the 'noble ones' (aryā), who are already walking the Noble Eightfold Path, and are progressing on to nirvāṇa, and those who are not yet on the path, the ordinary individuals, who must make efforts to become capable of one day reaching the path. For these more ordinary individuals, the path is often presented in a threefold version focused on developing moral conduct (*sīla*), meditation (*bhavānā*) and wisdom (*prajñā/paññā*). Again, these should not be seen necessarily as sequential steps, but as nurturing and supporting each other: wisdom and tranquil mind developed through meditation are necessary to adopt moral conduct, and moral conduct in turn sustains reflection and the development of wisdom. An individual's proximity to, and progression on, the path depends on the moral quality of his or her intentional behaviour in all aspects of his or her life. The awakened person actualizes the path in each and every action.

▶ Historical highlights: the arrival of Buddhism in Tibet

According to the traditional accounts, Buddhism first came to Tibet in the 7th century, when King Songtsen Gampo (died c. 650) built up the Tibetan empire that expanded for the next two centuries. He married two Buddhist princesses, one from China and the other from Nepal, who were said to have brought with them Buddhist artefacts and practices. However, the first diffusion of Buddhism did not happen until the 8th century under King Trisong Detsen (742-797) who reputedly invited the Indian scholar Śāntarakṣita from the great Buddhist monastic university of Nālandā to establish Buddhism in Tibet. His efforts were not initially successful and he had to call on the great miracle-worker Padmasambhava to subdue and convert Tibetan gods and demons through magic. Eventually, Śantarakṣita was able to build the first monastery at Samye. Under royal patronage, Buddhism was established as the state religion and, at least in royal circles, took hold against the indigenous Tibetan religious tradition, Bön, until the reign of King Langdarma who, according to the traditional account, wiped out monastic Buddhism from Tibet. It is not until the 11th century that Buddhism received broad royal support again, although it is believed that it developed among the people, mixing with indigenous practices.

The second diffusion of Buddhism started under King Yeshe Ö (c. 959–1040) who initiated a programme of translation and study by sending Tibetans to train in India,

▲ Figure 4.2 Padmasambhava, Lower Mustang, Nepal

and inviting Indian teachers to teach in Tibet. He is still revered today by Tibetans for having reputedly given up his life to ensure that the great Indian scholar Atiśa (982–1054) could stay in Tibet. Atiśa's legacy is both institutional and scholastic. His foremost disciple established the Kadam-pa school, a monastic tradition based on bringing together Madhyamaka philosophical principles and the Tantric tradition, and which distinguished itself with its emphasis on textual study and strict monastic discipline.

In addition to the Kadam-pa, and the Nyingma-pa (who traced their lineage to the first transmission and Padmasambhava), two other schools developed in the 11th and 12th centuries: the Sakya-pa and the Kagyu-pa. The last school to develop, the Gelug-pa, was founded by the scholar-monk Tsongkhapa (1357–1410) who sought to re-establish the Kadam-pa emphasis on the study of Madhyamaka philosophy and observance of strict monastic discipline.

In the 16th century, the head of the Gelug-pa was adopted as his spiritual teacher by the Mongol Alta Khan who gave him the title of Dalai Lama. The Mongol invaders established the fifth Dalai Lama as Tibet's ruler in 1641, a position that the Dalai Lamas kept up until 1959 when the present 14th Dalai Lama had to flee Tibet under Chinese control, although he was still the head of the government in exile until 2011, when he formally retired from the position.

In the 19th century, as a reaction to the political and, to a certain extent, doctrinal domination of the Gelug-pa, a non-sectarian (Rimé in Tibetan) movement advocating an eclectic approach to the study and practice of Buddhism brought together the Sakya-pa, Niyngma-pa and Kagyu-pa schools. In the 20th century the Rimé movement became increasingly successful due also to the support of prominent Tibetan religious leaders from all schools, including the 14th Dalai Lama.

In Tibet itself, from 1966, Buddhism was fiercely repressed during the long decade of the Chinese Cultural Revolution (1966-76). While there was a certain softening in the 1980s and 1990s, which allowed for resurgence, the political situation has been tense again since 2008, with periodical riots in Lhasa and other regions and violent incidents, including over 100 public self-immolations by monks and nuns.[30]

Rebirth, karma and merit-making

▶ Making offerings to the Three Jewels

Today is full moon, and Ning gets up early: she wants to give alms to the monks who go on alms-rounds every morning. She puts some fragrant jasmine rice on to steam, and prepares some curry. When the food is ready, she packs it into individual bags, and makes a quick stop to the covered food market to pick up fresh flowers and fruit. As she parks her motorbike in her courtyard, she notices the line of barefoot monks. She is just in time to get the offerings and wait in front of the house. The monks, in their saffron-coloured robes, their begging bowls held in front of them by a wide fabric strap, walk slowly. As they notice Ning waiting, they stop and face her, their gaze down. Their behaviour is strictly regulated by monastic rules, which they must respect at all times. Ning approaches and places a bag of rice, a bag of curry, and a mango and flower in each bowl. She then kneels in front of the monks, and bows her head slightly, holding her hands together while the monks chant a blessing. As soon as they are finished chanting, they walk away slowly. The whole ritual lasts less than a few minutes, and Ning goes back into her house before heading to the temple.

Connections

In Laos, and parts of Thailand where people are ethnic Lao, instead of going towards the standing monks, people usually put a mat down on the ground, take off their shoes, and wait for the monks to walk by them, putting food in their bowls as they walk pass.

Scattered on the street that borders the temple compound, street vendors selling flower arrangements that include three incense sticks, a candle, and a gold leaf wrapped in waxed paper jostle for Ning's custom. Before entering the main hall, she takes off her shoes and leaves them at the entrance. In Thailand, shoes are considered unclean and are usually not worn inside, and especially not anywhere where there are Buddha images. It is both a sign of respect to the Buddha and the monks, and a way of keeping the space free from dust and dirt.

Ning prostrates three times towards the main Buddha image sitting on the raised platform at the front of the sala, the main room, while reciting the refuge in the Three Jewels. She then lights the candle and the incense sticks and places them in front of the main Buddha, and rubs the gold leaf on the statue. Many have done the same thing and the statue is covered in gold. Around her, others engage in similar activities as they stream into the sala, parents showing young children how to prostrate themselves by placing palms together, raising them to the forehead, and to the chest, before putting them, along with elbows and forehead, on the floor. They are taught the Refuge prayer, and then are usually left free to play or sometimes even run around the sala. In Theravāda Buddhism, there are no set services in which adherents come together as a congregation, but people come in their own time, usually on observance days. While only the most devout will attend all observance days, Ning usually attends at least once a month on full moon day, and she also attends most festivals during the year, as they are particularly auspicious and meritorious (see 100 ideas section for a list of major festivals). Besides taking refuge and the five precepts, and making offerings to the Buddha and to the *Saṅgha*, she also makes merit by freeing animals. Outside the temple, there are several people who sell birds to be released. She buys a couple and releases them, offering the merit thereby gained for the benefit of all beings, and specifically of her parents.

Connections

Observance (*uposatha*) days are set according to the lunar calendar and fall on full moon, half-moon and new moon days. On full and new moon days, the monastic community gathers and confesses any transgression of the monastic rules before reciting them in full. On these days, the lay community usually follows the five precepts more closely, and usually tries to visit the local temple to make merit. Devout Chinese Buddhists will usually not eat any animal products, especially meat and fish, or drink alcohol on these days.

▶ Rebirth

Buddhists believe that this life is just one among innumerable lives that we have gone through and will go through, whether as human beings or as other kinds of beings, including animals, 'hungry ghosts', hell beings or gods. This is *saṃsāra*, the 'round of rebirth', the endless repetition of death and rebirth that all beings experience. At its most basic, *saṃsāra* has three main characteristics: it is endless, it is characterized by suffering, and the only way to escape from it is to achieve nirvāṅa. It is said that it consists of six main realms of existence, divided into lower and higher realms. The three lower realms include, in descending order, the animal realm, the hungry spirit realm and the hell realm. Existence in the lower realms is considered unfortunate and the result of unwholesome actions in previous lives and beings in those realms are subject to great suffering and have hardly any opportunity for spiritual development. By contrast, life in the higher realms, which include the gods (*devas*) and the higher gods (*brahmās*), is said to be fortunate and extremely pleasant, and the result of wholesome actions. However, because existence in those higher realms is so enjoyable, it is not conducive to spiritual development either. On the other hand, human rebirth, the first level of the higher realms, is considered to offer the best combination of suffering and pleasure to motivate one to seek release from *saṃsāra*.

It is important to stress that, in the Buddhist worldview, being constantly reborn is not desirable, because of the ultimate suffering associated with impermanence. Ultimate happiness and satisfaction cannot be found in *saṃsāra*: happiness is always limited and finite. Being reborn as a human being gives us the unique opportunity to realize this fundamental truth and to attain liberation.

❱ Karma

The process of rebirth is not random. The realm and the circumstances in which one is reborn depend on the nature and quality of one's actions, what is called *karma*. The term *karma* has been widely adopted in Western languages such as English and French, but its original meaning has been distorted in the process. At its most basic, karma is intentional action, and the results of such action. In the West, karma is often understood merely as circumstances that result from past actions and therefore as deterministic, but the Buddhist understanding focuses primarily on the actions performed in the present rather than the circumstances resulting from past actions. In this way, the theory of karma clearly stresses the ability to act out of free will: even if we cannot change the circumstances we are born into, we can change our present actions and therefore affect our future circumstances.

According to Buddhist thought, we constantly perform actions of body, speech and mind (thoughts are also included in the concept of actions). These actions are divided into two basic types: wholesome and unwholesome. Wholesome actions lead to the well-being of self and others, and unwholesome actions lead to the opposite. It must be noted that the quality of an action is not determined by an outside party, such as a god, but rather it is inherent in the action itself based on the motivation that led it to be performed and its results. The traditional image is that of a seed and the tree that grows out of the seed: a peach stone will grow into a peach tree and bear peaches, just as a wholesome action will bear pleasant consequences, and an unwholesome one will bear unpleasant consequences. Wholesome actions are based on three positive roots or motivations: generosity, friendliness and wisdom. On the contrary, unwholesome actions are based on the three negative roots: greed, hatred and delusion.

The circumstances and nature of an individual's future rebirth are therefore conditioned by the actions that he or she performs in each lifetime. However, Buddhists also believe that some consequences of our actions are borne out in this very life.

Connections: karma, *saṃsāra* and the Four Noble Truths

The concepts of *saṃsāra* and *karma* (Pāli: *kamma*) are clearly related to the Noble Truths discussed in Chapter 4. The cycle of existence, *saṃsāra*, is suffering – this is the First Noble Truth. Our actions, especially unwholesome actions based on the three negative motivations, are the cause of suffering – the Second Noble Truth. Karma is what keeps us in *saṃsāra*, and while wholesome actions also have consequences, their ultimate positive consequence is to find oneself in a situation in which one can achieve nirvāṇa – the Third Noble Truth, and the way to develop these wholesome actions based on the three positive motivations is the Noble Eightfold Path – the Fourth Noble Truth.

◗ Merit-making

In fact, the Noble Eightfold Path could be described as a 'how to' guide to develop wholesome motivations. However, for many traditional Buddhists, it is also considered to be a 'how to' guide for those who are already spiritually advanced. More ordinary people have to take baby steps to develop wholesome actions, and these usually start with the threefold gradual scheme of developing virtuous conduct (*sīla*), calm mind (*bhāvanā*) and wisdom (*prajñā/ paññā*). Essentially, merit-making activities, such as those Ning is engaged in during morning alms-giving and the temple visit described above, fulfil two main functions. The first, and usually most obvious, is to improve one's present life and, eventually, future lives. The second function, which is at the heart of Buddhist thought, but may not always be explicitly stated, especially in popular practices, is to develop wholesome motivations. According to Buddhist psychology, the more we repeat an action, the more likely we are to engage in it, just as a path often travelled on becomes more and more easily accessible. It may be worthwhile noting that Western psychology is now coming to the same conclusion, and many books on how to break bad habits and develop new good ones[31] rest on ideas that have been part of Buddhist psychology for over 2,000 years.

Every Buddhist tradition has developed specific ways of making merit, but the major focus of merit-making centres on giving the basic requisites (food, clothing, shelter and medicine) to the monastic community. As we have seen above, in Theravādin societies, monks still carry out the canonical requirement of going on alms-rounds in the community. Even in non-traditionally Buddhist societies, like North America, where it may be difficult to go on alms-rounds, monks at local temples still depend on alms, and community members will organize rotas to ensure that the monks are brought food on a daily basis. In Chinese Buddhism, the laity often sponsors meals for the monks and nuns of an entire monastery, including its preparation in the monastery kitchen. Offerings also include robes for the monks, usually given during the *Katina* ceremony in Theravāda Buddhism (see the 100 ideas section for festivals), donations of money, labour and materials for building temples, stupas, and accommodations for the monks. Sponsoring the printing and dissemination of Buddhist teachings is a merit-making activity that is particularly widespread in Chinese Buddhism.

▲ Figure 5.1 Food offering to monks, Kanchanaburi, Thailand

Connections

The greatest merit obviously is gained by devoting one's life to developing the Eightfold Path, by becoming a monk or a nun. However, not everyone can make this level of commitment and, in Thailand, men and boys often ordain for a short period, from a day to a year. It is widely accepted that the merit thus gained is for the benefit of one's parents, especially one's mother, because women cannot receive full ordination and therefore gain the merit for themselves. This is changing, however, as women and girls are given the same opportunity by the first fully ordained Thai *bhikkhunī*, Dhammananda.[32]

▶ Syncretic practices

The different Buddhist traditions have assimilated many non-Buddhist rituals, such as the Chinese cult of the ancestors, or the Lao and Thai agricultural and spirit propitiating rites, by integrating them within the merit-making activities and inserting the *Saṅgha* as the operative intermediary. For example, in a Lao ceremony involving the feeding of deceased ancestors and relatives, special foods prepared for the ancestors are left on temple grounds, and alms-food is offered to the monks who, symbolically, transfer the merit thus gained to the deceased. Another example is that of an agricultural ritual propitiating the rice-field spirit and in which the tradition recounts that the recipient of the propitiatory offerings requested that they be made to the monks instead. It is believed that it is only through the monks, who should observe a pure and dedicated lifestyle, that the rites are made efficacious.[33]

These various activities, and the transference of merit that they imply, from the living to the deceased, from sons to mothers, from monks to supernatural spirits, have sometimes caused confusion and questioning among non-Buddhists, especially in light of the law of karma in which one is singly and uniquely responsible for one's past and present actions and therefore for their consequences. However, they are best viewed as representing the development of *sīla*, moral conduct and especially *dāna*, the virtue of generosity. Giving, whether it is food and robes to the monks, offerings to spirits and the deceased, freedom to caged animals, or merit to one's parents or deceased relatives, is a way of developing the virtue of generosity, a virtue that is presented as the foundation of all other virtues. Psychologically, generosity helps us to open up to others, to realize that all beings are part of the same cycle of existence, bound by karma to *saṃsāra*, and subject to suffering in the same way that we are.

6

Meditation

▶ Sitting zazen

This week, Haruki is attending a *sesshin*, a period of intensive meditation during which the monks sit in *zazen* for long sessions and limit other activities. Traditionally, a sign is hung on the monastery door to let lay devotees and visitors know not to distract the monks. During *sesshin*, monks alternate periods of sitting meditation with short periods of walking meditation (*kinhin*) throughout the day. The aim of the *sesshin* is to intensify the training, and provide an extended period during which there are few or no distractions, and the sole focus is to develop concentration and awareness. During *sesshin*, speaking, looking around and common social interactions are strictly limited to maximize mental concentration and limit disruptions. The way of executing even the smallest action, such as entering the hall or sitting down, is precisely stipulated, and requires great attention. Haruki enters on the left side of the entrance, left foot first. After two steps, he bows in *gassho*, hands joined together in front of his face, forearms parallel to the floor, elbows away from the body. He then walks to his seat on the elevated platform, bows towards the seat, and turns to his right until he is facing the other side of the room and bows again. He sits down on the cushion on the platform, avoiding touching with his feet or buttocks the wooden border where meals are served, and turns right again until he faces the wall. He sways gently right and left, front and back, to settle down and find the right balance, holds his gaze with eyes slightly downcast, and waits for the three bells that announce the beginning of *zazen*. He inhales and exhales through his mouth once, and then starts breathing through his nose naturally, counting each breath until ten, and then starting again. In Rinzai Zen, meditators are given a *kōan* to focus on, but in Sōtō Zen, meditators usually focus on the breath. The bell is struck twice to indicate the start of *kinhin*. After getting up from the cushion in the same manner as he sat down, Haruki folds his hands in *shashu*, the right hand covering the left fist, and held on his chest, and takes a step. Each step must last a full breath, and the heel must strike the ground slowly, just level with the toes of the other foot. After ten minutes, the bell is struck three times again, and *zazen* resumes, only interrupted briefly for meals and short rest periods.

▶ Buddhist meditation

In the Western mind, Buddhism often evokes images of serene monks and nuns sitting cross-legged for lengthy periods in a state of deep trance. Indeed, activities that promote concentration, awareness and attention are fundamental to the Buddhist path. The English term 'meditation' is often used to translate several Sanskrit and Pāli terms and, in particular, *bhāvanā*, which is part of the threefold scheme that also includes good conduct and wisdom (discussed in Chapters 4 and 5). The term *bhāvanā* means 'developing' or 'cultivating', implying developing positive states of mind, in particular the wholesome motivations of generosity, friendliness and wisdom that are conducive to the accomplishment of the path. But this is not an easy task because the mind, in its unawakened and undeveloped state, is considered to be difficult to control. It is constantly distracted by a thought, a sensation, a feeling, an emotion. Despite our best intentions, resolutions to remain focused are constantly disturbed, disrupted, and soon forgotten. A traditional metaphor compares the mind to a glass of water that has been mixed up with mud. Only when the glass is left tranquil and unmoved for a period of time, will the mud settle at the bottom of the glass, leaving the water untroubled. Meditation, it is argued, allows the troubled waters of our thoughts, feelings and emotions to settle down letting our minds become still and untroubled, and therefore regaining their original purity and clarity. Based on this primary step, essentially two main alternatives have developed in the Buddhist tradition: calm meditation and insight meditation, the main features of which underlie most of the meditation techniques of all Buddhist traditions.

Calm meditation

The practice of calm meditation (*samatha*) is concerned with developing tranquillity and stilling the mind. In the Theravāda tradition, Buddhaghosa, a 5th century monk, described 40 objects of meditation that correspond to different meditators' character types and levels of competence. An object of meditation therefore should be chosen according to the individual meditator. This is usually done by the teacher: most Buddhist traditions emphasize the importance of the spiritual teacher who guides the meditator. In fact, the original Sanskrit and Pāli term for spiritual teacher, *kalyāṇamitra/kalyāṇamitta*, means 'good friend' and, in an early text, the Buddha himself is shown as the perfect example of the 'good friend' who frees those who rely on him from suffering.

The 40 objects can be material or mental objects and can be roughly organized into six main categories of meditator types. Some, such as the *kasiṇas* representing the four elements of earth, fire, water and air, are suitable for all meditator types. Others are more suitable for the meditator types dominated by the three negative roots of greed, hatred and delusion. For example, those of hateful disposition are given to meditate on colour *kasiṇas*, discs of colours representing the three primary colours and white, or on the four immeasurable qualities of loving kindness, compassion, sympathetic joy and equanimity. Those of greedy disposition are given to meditate on the processes of decomposition of corpses, or mindfulness of the body. Those of delusional disposition can meditate on mindfulness of breathing. Other objects of meditation, such as the recollections of the Buddha, Dharma and *Saṅgha*, or positive qualities such as good conduct and generosity, are suitable for those of trustful disposition, while still others, such as the mindfulness of death, or recollection of peace, are suitable for those of intellectual temperament.

One develops mindfulness of the chosen object of meditation by focusing attention on it, and bringing attention back to it every time it flits away. Being mindful means observing with attention, but without judgement. One notes when the mind moves away from the object of meditation, and relentlessly brings it back, without reacting to it as a good or a bad thing. As one develops this ability to stay on the object of meditation, the mind becomes focused and composed, attaining a state of concentration (*samādhi*). Bearing in mind the metaphor of the glass of water, focusing the mind on an object, whether material or mental, and constantly bringing it back to it, allows the mud of our thoughts, feelings and emotions to settle slowly and leaves the mind pure and clear.

As the mind becomes more and more focused, higher levels of concentration are achieved, in which the mind is very still and very focused. Even higher stages are said to parallel the cosmological realms of the *brahmās*, the higher gods. Fundamentally, psychological states parallel cosmological planes: calm meditation allows us to 'taste' life in the gods' realms, just as the emotions of anger or hatred allow us to 'taste' life in the lower realms.

Connections: the five hindrances

The obstacles, listed in Buddhist texts, that one encounters in meditation, and also often when simply trying to focus on a task:

1 Sensual desire: the meditator is continuously distracted by the six senses (including the mind), and yearns for sense stimuli such as food or entertainment.

2 Ill-will: the meditator starts resenting and rejecting the meditation practice, finding fault with it in countless respects.

3 Tiredness and lethargy: the meditator becomes lethargic, and may even fall asleep during meditation.

4 Restlessness and anxiety: the meditator is excited at the thought of some success in meditation, or anxious about success.

5 Doubt: the meditator starts questioning the value, use and purpose of the practice.

Insight meditation

Calm meditation is often described as a preliminary to insight meditation, and it is certain that a deep level of concentration is necessary to develop insight. Fundamentally, both calm and insight are necessary to achieve nirvāṇa. One of the foundational texts describing the development of insight is the *Mahāsatipaṭṭhāna Sutta* in the Long Discourses of the Buddha in the Pāli canon. In this text, mindfulness is applied to four categories of phenomena: the body, feelings, mental states and finally the basic physical and mental phenomena (*dharmas/dhammas* - see Chapter 8) that comprise our experience of the world. The meditator is enjoined to focus on the breath and all the sensations that arise in the body when sitting in meditation. When moving, such as when the Zen meditators above engage in *kinhin*, the meditator focuses on the sensations arising from the movements, noting as they arise, stay and fade away. This can be applied to all movements one performs throughout the day. The same process is applied to the feelings that arise; the meditator should observe them as they arise and fade continuously, noting their presence and whether they are pleasant, unpleasant or neutral, whether they arise from the body or the mind. When observing the mind, the *sutta* focuses particularly on noting the presence or absence of the three negative motivations in the mind. As the meditation becomes more refined, the focus shifts to the five aggregates (*skandhas/khandhas* - see Chapter 8) and how they arise and cease, and furthermore to specific phenomena such as the five hindrances or the seven factors associated with awakening such as mindfulness, perseverance, serenity and concentration. The meditator continues to observe how these arise and fade in the mind. Finally, the *sutta* describes how the meditator examines the Four Noble Truths exhaustively leading eventually to awakening.

Insight meditation develops non-attachment and wisdom into the true nature of all phenomena: that they are impermanent, unsatisfactory and not-Self (that is, a true, eternal, element that can be identified as one's own self cannot be found in any phenomenon). This process of examination starts with the grosser aspects of the body and moves to more and more subtle phenomena including, the *khandhas*, the dimensions of one's personality that are often mistaken for oneself (the body, feelings, perceptions, volitional formations, and consciousness). These too are to be recognized as impermanent and unsatisfactory, which makes them a fundamentally inadequate repository for a Self. While this can be understood intellectually, it is not sufficient, and meditation allows it to be experienced, realized and internalized. This experiential understanding leads to the ultimate realization of nirvāṇa.

▲ Figure 6.1 Meditation Hall, Japan

▶ Developments in Northern and Eastern Buddhisms

It can be fairly argued that the very diverse meditation practices that can be found in the Buddhist world are an expression of either calm or insight meditation, and often a combination of both with varying emphases. Visualizations in Tibetan Buddhism draw on Tantric practices, but they still rely on establishing concentration on one's tutelary deity (*yi-dam*) with actions of body through ritual gestures (*mudrās*), speech with the recitation of the deity's *mantras*, and mind through visualization of the deity and his or her Pure Land (*maṇḍala*).

Another focus of Tibetan Buddhist meditation is the generation of the *bodhicitta*, the mind of awakening. This is done through structured meditations that develop a sense of equanimity and compassion towards all sentient beings, for example, meditating that through the cycle of endless rebirths, every single being has been, at one point or another, one's mother. Another meditation involves 'exchanging self with other', realizing that one's aspirations and fears are the same as others' aspirations and fears. This eventually will lead to the generation of great compassion that will motivate one to engage on the Bodhisattva path to attain awakening for the benefit of all sentient beings.

Pure Land Buddhism focuses on activities of devotion to Buddha Amitābha, including prostrations, the recitation of the *nianfo*, a short salutation to Amitābha, and visualization of his Pure Land, but it emphasizes complete faith in the power of Amitābha's vows to achieve the goal: according to Pure Land Buddhism, the devotee cannot achieve anything by his or her own power (self-power) and must have total faith in Amitābha's power (other-power), a drastic evolution from the approach of a text like the *Mahāsatipaṭṭhāna Sutta*, in which the meditator brings about his or her own realization.

Chan meditation (the term is a translation of the Sanskrit *dhyāna* – a state of profound meditative absorption) developed in China and split into two main schools. The Linji school (Japanese Rinzai) argues that awakening already exists and cannot be produced by spiritual practices, and therefore is 'sudden'. As a result, it promotes the use of *gong an* (Japanese *kōan*), paradoxical statements one must meditate upon to allow awakening to become manifest. The Caodong school (Japanese Sōtō), on the other hand, propounds a gradual path to awakening and emphasizes 'just sitting' meditation as we have seen above at Haruki's monastery.

▶ Some developments in Western countries

Since the late 1970s, Buddhist meditation, especially mindfulness (*vipassanā*), has been introduced in mainstream culture as a technique to improve physical and mental health. It has been used in psychotherapeutic contexts, for example as a way to develop awareness of feelings, emotions and motivations, and to improve psychotherapeutic outcomes. In England, the Karuna Institute[34] was founded in 1984 to offer training in psychotherapy based on Buddhist ideals, such as compassion (Skt: *karunā*), and meditation techniques such as Theravāda-based mindfulness, and Tibetan medical tantric Kum Nye. In the healthcare and medical fields, meditation techniques, often stripped of their religious and cultural characteristics, are used to alleviate a variety of medical symptoms, including high blood pressure, chronic pain, stress, and low immune function. A North American example of this is the work of Jon Kabat-Zinn, who developed a Mindfulness-Based Stress Reduction programme that is widely used in healthcare.[35] Buddhist meditation techniques are also used in a broad range of activities aiming at increasing overall physical and mental 'wellness' in the workplace, relationships, and personal life. For example, the work of Stanford University-based Center for Compassion and Altruism Research and Education (CCARE)[36] and of the Mind & Life Institute[37] also seek to find ways of improving personal and societal well-being by integrating Buddhist concepts and techniques with Western scientific methodology. Another aspect of this trend is how companies, such as Facebook,[38] are incorporating broadly Buddhistic approaches into their organizational values and practices or, as Google, inviting Buddhist masters such as Thich Nath Hanh,[39] or meditation teachers such as Jon Kabat-Zinn,[40] to their headquarters to train their staff.

This mainstreaming of Buddhist ideas and practices in society has caused some excitement and enthusiasm, but also words of caution as, clearly, we are far from the conception of meditation (or compassion) as the path of renouncement propounded by the Buddha to achieve the 'letting go of craving and the end of rebirth'. Some Buddhist practitioners have argued against this instrumentalization of Buddhist ideas and practices for worldly objectives. It is an ongoing process and it will surely be interesting to see how it evolves in the long term and what impact it will have on society at large and on Buddhism.

Faith and devotion

▶ Jin Yen

Jin Yen wakes every morning at 5 a.m. for her devotional practice. After getting dressed and tidying her room, all of which she seeks to accomplish mindfully, she bows her head to the altar placed above her desk in her room, then bows deeply three times, her upper body at a straight angle, before standing up and bowing again. She then places a bowl of water, and lights a stick of incense, as offerings to the Buddha image she has set up on her desk. She bows again once to the altar. She then makes a bow in homage to the historical Buddha, Śākyamuni. She then bows paying homage to Amitābha Buddha, and then chanting the *nianfo*, the homage verse to Amitābha, while performing 48 full prostrations, an extended form of bowing that requires kneeling and touching the floor with her forehead, with her hands, palms up, next to her knees. When she has finished her prostrations, she bows again, before sitting down and chanting the *Diamond Sūtra* for 15 minutes, and then meditating on the Pure Land of Amitābha Buddha for another 15 minutes. At the end of her meditation, she stands up, bows to the Bodhisattvas Guanyin and Daishizhi, and to all the Bodhisattvas. She then makes repentance for the harm she has caused, and vows to be reborn in the Pure Land of Amitābha, before dedicating the merit of her practice to all living beings.

▶ Faith

Buddhism is often perceived as a 'rational' religion whose founder did not require blind faith from his followers, but advised them in the often-quoted *Sutta to the Kālāmas* not to follow tradition, or scriptures, or even a teacher, but to 'know for themselves' by examining every teaching thoroughly. Yet, faith and devotion are an important part of Buddhist practice and, in fact, faith (*śraddhā/saddhā*) is the first step on the path for, if one had no faith in the Buddha, his teachings and the community he established, one would not be inclined even to consider them. The future Buddha himself is shown expressing his faith in the former Buddha, and thence starting his path to Buddhahood, and the common description of one who becomes a follower of the Buddha in the Pāli texts always includes how it starts with establishing faith in the Buddha. In this context, faith is trust that the Buddha was truly awakened, and that putting his teachings into practice will truly lead one to awakening or, to put it another way, faith is trust that following the path will lead one to realize directly the truth of what one had faith in to start with. Faith, in Buddhist thought, therefore intrinsically implies a basic level of practice, which takes the form of devotional practices which, ideally, help to increase faith and thus motivate further practice in a self-sustaining virtuous circle. At present and, as shown by textual and archaeological evidence, historically, faith and devotion have been the main focus of religious life for the majority of people in traditional Buddhist cultures.

▶ Devotion

There is a large range of devotional practices in Buddhism that may appear unrelated, but many are based on a number of fundamental practices common to all traditions that focus on activities of body, speech and mind, deliberately engaging the whole person in the devotional practice.

The Refuge prayer is the formal expression of one's commitment to the 'Three Jewels': the Buddha (the one who shows the path), the Dharma (the teachings) and the *Saṅgha* (the community of those who follow the Buddhist path). By reciting the Refuge prayer, one becomes a Buddhist or, on a regular basis, reiterates one's faith in, and commitment to, the Buddhist path. Refuge prayers vary according to the traditions, but their focus remains the Three Jewels. Other prayers, formulas and *sūtras* are also chanted as part of devotional activities.

▲ Figure 7.1 Tibetan man with prayer wheel, Bodhgayā, India

Connections

The Pāli Refuge prayer, which Therāvada Buddhists recite, consists of these sentences repeated three times: 'I go for refuge to the Buddha, I go for refuge to the Dharma, I go for refuge to the Saṅgha.'

Bowing is a way of showing respect and appreciation in Asian cultures. All devotional activities incorporate bowing in one form or another, from a standing bow in which one inclines only the head, to full body prostration. Bows and prostrations are directed to the Buddha and Bodhisattvas, and to one's spiritual teachers.

Connections

Tibetan Buddhists have different versions of the Refuge prayer. The simpler one is the same as the Pāli prayer, but usually adds as a first line: 'I go for refuge to the guru.' Another common Refuge prayer refers to all Buddhas and emphasizes that awakening is to be obtained, not just for oneself, but for the benefit of all: 'Until I reach awakening, I take refuge in all the Buddhas and in the Dharma and all the Noble Saṅgha. By the merit of accomplishing the six perfections, may I achieve Buddhahood for the benefit of all sentient beings.'

Making offerings to Buddha and Bodhisattva images is also a way to show devotion. In most Buddhist homes, there is a more or less elaborate shrine, sometimes a

Buddha image on a simple shelf placed high on a wall, other times, a more elaborate arrangement with images of Buddhas and Bodhisattvas, and photographs of teachers, which is the focus of home-based devotion. There are no set times (unlike mass for example), but devout Buddhists will usually offer incense, flowers and lights to the Buddha on a daily basis, with more elaborate offerings on special occasions such as observance days in Theravāda Buddhism. In Tibetan Buddhism, water is also used as an offering to symbolize various material and spiritual offerings (Chapter 4). In Pure Land Buddhism as practised by Jin Yen above, water is said to symbolize the purity and tranquility of the mind, and placing it on the altar helps remind the devotee of the true nature of the mind. In Thai temples, as we saw in Chapter 5, devotees apply gold leaf to the Buddha images in the temple. Other offerings include Buddha images, land and material for temple and monastic buildings, food for the monastic community, and adornments for the temples, including stupas, and frescoes and paintings of the life of the Buddha for example.

Going on pilgrimages is also an act of devotion. In Pāli texts, the Buddha enjoins his followers to visit the places where he was born, attained awakening, delivered his first sermon and where he will pass away. He also advises that his relics be enshrined in stupas, so that people can worship there too. Stupas are also built as a special act of devotion, and monastery grounds often contain numerous stupas of varying sizes and ages. Traditionally stupas contain relics of the Buddha, and of Buddhist saints (those believed to have realized awakening) and scriptures.

▲ Figure 7.2 Circumambulating the Bodhnath stupa, with pilgrim prostrating, Kathmandu, Nepal

In the *Mahāparinibbāna Sutta*, the Buddha tells Ānanda what is to be done with his bodily remains:

'A stupa should be raised for the Buddha at a crossroads. And whoever brings to that place garlands or incense or sandalpaste, or pay reverence, and whose mind becomes calm there – it will be to their well-being and happiness for a long time ... At the thought: "This is the stupa of that Blessed One, Arahant, Fully Awakened One!" the hearts of many people will be calmed and made happy.'

Circumambulating of stupas, temples and Bodhi-trees is another activity of devotion engaging mind, body and speech as one walks around, with mind fully focused, and chanting a verse or a mantra. In Tibetan Buddhism, a common way of circumambulation is by doing full prostrations around the building. Devotees wear special knee pads and wooden pads on their hands to protect them as they slide down on the ground. An important place for Tibetan Buddhists is the residence of the Dalai Lama which they circumambulate while chanting '*Oṃ Maṇi Padme Hūṃ*', the mantra of Avalokiteśvara, the Bodhisattva of whom the Dalai Lama is said to be an emanation.

▶ Devotion and the Buddhist path

It will be noticed, at this point, that devotion and the practice of the Buddhist path become one and the same.

Devotion in Buddhism is not antithetical to the path; on the contrary, all devotional activities are more than just preliminaries to the Buddhist path – they are ways to engage on the path at one's own level. Offerings are a way to practise good conduct (*sīlā*) by developing generosity (*dāna*). Chanting, bowing and circumambulating bring together the body, speech and mind and, especially when done with full concentration, involve the development of the qualities necessary in meditation (*bhāvanā*). Reflecting on the Buddha's qualities as part of devotional practices also helps to develop a sense of the Eightfold Path and of the true nature of existence, and therefore of wisdom.

A variety of activities emphasizing different aspects also appeal to different kinds of people, therefore ensuring that everyone can access the path from the place they are at. It is recognized that not everyone has the spiritual capacity (or desire) to dedicate his or her life entirely to the pursuit of nirvāṇa, nor to engage in lengthy meditation practices, or in the intense study of the Dharma either due to one's own failings or to surrounding circumstances, but that devotional activities are accessible to all beings and that, if done with a pure and focused mind, can even lead one to the goal itself.

▶ Pure Land and Nichiren

Pure Land Buddhism in China and Japan, as well as Nichiren, a later Japanese development, deserve special mention because of their unique focus on faith and devotion as the only means of salvation. As discussed in Chapter 6, in China, Jingtu or Pure Land Buddhism focuses on the worship of Buddha Amitābha and on achieving rebirth in his Pure Land. It promoted a range of practices to achieve this goal and emphasized complete faith in the power of Amitābha's vows (other-power) meanwhile denying that the devotee could do anything to attain the goal (self-power).

In Japan, Pure Land teachings took the concept of other-power a step further when Hōnen promoted the recitation of the *nembutsu*, the salutation to Amitābha (Jap: Amida), and his disciple Shinran rejected all spiritual practices except for the *nembutsu*, arguing that there was nothing one could do to achieve rebirth in the Pure Land and was entirely dependent on the grace of Amitābha. A similar attitude was taken by Nichiren who saw the *Lotus Sūtra* as the final and fullest teaching of the Buddha, and complete devotion to the *Lotus Sūtra* and the recitation of the invocation 'Homage to the *Lotus Sūtra* of the True Dharma' as the only correct form of practice.

8

Buddhist philosophy

▶ A Tibetan puja

Robert aims to spend regular periods of time studying Buddhist philosophical texts. At the moment, he is reading a translation of Śantideva's *Bodhicaryāvatāra*, an 8th century text that describes the development of *bodhicitta* - the awakening mind. The *Bodhicaryāvatāra* touches upon many ideas of Mahāyāna Buddhism, and is also described by some scholars as a meditation manual that explains how to develop the awakening mind. He also attends *pujas* which, in the Tibetan tradition, are rituals focusing on one particular Buddha or Bodhisattva. Commonly performed pujas are the Medicine Buddha Puja (*Bhaiṣajyaguru*) or the Green Tara Puja, as they are believed to help heal diseases and overcome obstacles. Before entering the temple's main room, Robert leaves his shoes on a rack by the entrance. From the door, he takes in the seated Buddha image flanked on his left by Tsongkhapa, the founder of the Gelug-pa school of Tibetan Buddhism, which Robert follows and, on his right, Maitreya the future Buddha. Above and around the main images, a multitude of Bodhisattva and Buddha statues have been placed, most of them bedecked with *kathas*, white silk scarves that Tibetans give and receive as auspicious symbols. Below the images, several more or less ornate chairs have been arranged on the platform that lines the wall. A framed portrait of His Holiness the Dalai Lama stands on the most sumptuous throne-like chair, just below the main Buddha image. The temple boasts a spacious room where several people are already sitting on meditation cushions, some with texts placed in front of them on wooden stands. *Thangkas*, ornate Tibetan paintings usually representing

Buddhas and Bodhisattvas, adorn the pale yellow walls. On each side of the altar, and on the back wall, niches contain sacred texts.

Gathering his mind, Robert prostrates three times towards the altar raising his joined hands to the crown of his head, then to his throat, and to his heart, before kneeling and touching his head to the ground. He then assumes the half-lotus position on a cushion. A few monks and nuns, resident at the monastery, enter the room, and sit at the front after prostrating. The puja starts with chanting homage to the Buddhas, Bodhisattvas and teachers. At regular intervals, bells and drums are struck. The participants make symbolic offerings and chant the 21 praises to Tara, while visualizing Tara bestowing her blessings onto them, and eventually visualizing

▲ Figure 8.1 Tara Puja, Tharig Gompa, Boudha, Nepal

themselves as Tara. Robert remembers hearing a lama describing a puja as a way of welcoming the deities and the qualities that they represent into one's body, speech and mind by bringing these together while performing the ritual. As the chanting subsides, everyone remains in a moment of silent meditation.

Connections

Mahāyāna refers to a diverse range of concepts and practices within Buddhism that started developing in the 1st century BCE. In the popular, and even scholarly, imagination, Mahāyāna Buddhism emerged as a widespread lay movement in Classical India. However, the latest scholarship shows that in fact the Mahāyāna arose as a conservative monastic movement that concerned only a limited number of monks and nuns for several centuries. Indeed, despite a very substantial production of texts that started as early as the 1st century BCE, it seems probable that the earliest inscriptional evidence clearly and explicitly referring to the Mahāyāna as such, dates from as late as the 5th century.

▶ The rise of the Mahāyāna

The rise of the Mahāyāna can be attributed to a constellation of factors. On the one hand, the death of the Buddha left a void that was exacerbated by the philosophical stance that the Buddha was no longer accessible, and this seemed to contradict the notion of a compassionate Buddha who had achieved awakening for the benefit of all beings. On the other hand, meditative practices focusing on recollection of the Buddha (*buddhānusmṛti*) and relic worship entailed the notion that the Buddha was somehow still present, still accessible, and that one could still receive teachings from him. The idea that the Buddha was accessible, and still teaching are found in Mahāyāna sutras, such as the highly influential *Lotus Sūtra* (*Saddharmapuṇḍarīka Sūtra*), in which the Buddha elucidates his transcendental nature: his life as Siddhartha Gautama was an instance of 'skilful means' and, in fact, he had already attained awakening incalculable eons ago and taught innumerable beings.[41] He further claims his continuous and everlasting presence: 'My lifespan is immeasurable and incalculable. I abide forever without entering ultimate nirvāṇa.'

Mahāyāna distinguished itself as the 'great' or 'superior' path to salvation, in opposition to what it perceived to be a *hīnayāna*, a 'lower' or 'inferior' path. (It is necessary to clarify that the *hīnayāna* as described by Mahāyāna texts is not the path of the Theravāda. Using the term *hīnayāna* to describe the Theravāda is derogatory.) This claim to superiority was based on a variety of ideas and practices, but three main ideas are common to the majority of Mahāyāna movements:

Buddhahood is the preferred goal: Mahāyānists saw mainstream nirvāṇa-seeking Buddhists as selfish, and themselves as seeking full Buddhahood for the benefit of all beings.

The Bodhisattva path, the long and extraordinary quest pursued by the historical Buddha which is told in numerous *Jātakas* (stories of the Buddha's previous lives), is now not just the precinct of a very few, unique and exceptional individuals, but is the true Buddhist path that all should endeavour to follow.

A set of three concepts becomes predominant in Mahāyāna: compassion (*karunā*) for all beings, wisdom (*prajñā*) and skilful means (*upāya*)

The disparate groups that came to be included under the Mahāyāna umbrella developed cults around specific *sūtras* and Buddhas and Bodhisattvas. These practices became the focus of East Asian Buddhism with indigenous schools devoted to the *Lotus Sūtra*, or the *Avataṃsaka Sūtra*, and the worship of Amitābha Buddha and the Bodhisattva Avalokiteśvara (Chinese: Guanyin).

Connections

The term 'dharma' (Pāli: dhamma) encompasses three related meanings that need to be differentiated: 'Dharma', typically written with a capital 'D' in English, refers on the one hand to the way things truly are and, on the other, to the teaching of the Buddha – which elucidates how things truly are and how one can gain such an understanding. The term 'dharma', written with a lower-case 'd', and often in the plural, refers to the most basic material and mental elements that make up the world and, in the final analysis, is what the world and our experience truly are.

▶ Early Buddhist philosophy

At its most basic, Buddhist philosophy is concerned with describing the way things are. The description of the world, and how we experience it, was systematized in the Abhidharma (Pāli: Abhidhamma), the third basket of the canon which includes the 'higher' or 'further teachings' and which the legend tells us the Buddha imparted to an assembly of gods in a divine realm after his awakening. The Abhidharma represents an exhaustive attempt at analysing reality and human experience down to its smallest, irreducible constituents (*dharma/dhamma*), which are like the basic building blocks of reality. There are three main groups of *dharmas*: consciousness (bare awareness), mental factors (such as greed or friendliness) and physical phenomena (matter and related characteristics, such as softness or hardness).

Connections: the 12 links of dependent arising

'Conditioned by (1) ignorance are (2) [volitional] formations, conditioned by [volitional] formations is (3) consciousness, conditioned by consciousness is (4) mind-and-body [...], conditioned by mind-and-body are (5) the six senses, conditioned by the six senses is (6) sense-contact, conditioned by sense-contact is (7) feeling, conditioned by feeling is (8) craving, conditioned by craving is (9) attachment (or grasping), conditioned by attachment is (10) becoming, conditioned by becoming is (11) birth, conditioned by birth is (12) old age and death.'[42]

Buddhist philosophy focuses mainly on the nature of these *dharmas/dhammas*, and their relationship, which is explained by the concept of dependent arising (*pratītya-samutpāda/paṭiccasumuppāda*). The concept of dependent arising, according to which every aspect of our phenomenal experience is causally connected to previous factors themselves connected to previous factors in an infinite chain of causation, relates the way our experience arises to the Four Noble Truths and, in particular, to the claim that there is no such thing as a 'Self'.

▶ Not-self

All aspects of our experience are 'not-Self' (*anātman/anattā*), and what we take to be our 'self' is analysed into five psycho-physical constituents, the five *skandhas* (Pāli: *khandhas*), which comprise the totality of our experience. Based on matter (our body and the physical world), we experience feelings and perceptions that give rise to diverse reactions, such as desire, rejection or indifference, that impel us to act. Put simply, the 'we' that experiences is consciousness. These five constituents are explained as the basis for grasping, clinging and therefore suffering (First Noble Truth), and they do not constitute a self understood as a permanent, unchangeable and free-from-suffering entity, since none of them is permanent, unchangeable and free from suffering.

Connections: the five constituents (*skandhas/khandhas*)

Matter includes the four elements: earth, water, fire and wind, and what is dependent upon them. It encompasses the interactions between the material world and human consciousness.

Feelings include six kinds of feelings based on the six senses (sight, hearing, taste, smell, touch and mind). They consist of basic reactions to experience that can be pleasant, unpleasant or neutral, which quality may influence subsequent responses.

Perception implies the idea of recognition or conceptualization, for example of a colour as a specific colour, or of an object as a specific kind of object.

Volitional formations have an intentional quality and a conditioning influence on our thoughts and actions.

Consciousness is aware: aware of an object (physical or mental) and of the feelings, reactions and intentions it induces.

The five constituents and the links of dependent arising essentially describe how entangled we are with the world and our experience of, and reaction to, it. This is to be contrasted to the way things truly are, i.e. basic elements that continually arise and cease to be. What we take to be a real, unchanging, permanent self is a collection of such causally connected basic elements, constantly evolving and reconfiguring themselves. One possible metaphor is that of a river that appears the same and, yet, is constantly made up of flowing water, mud, stones and aquatic creatures.

▶ The Madhyamaka

In early Buddhist thought, the basic elements that form reality are held to exist despite their transience and absence of inherent self, that is they exist independently of whether someone apprehends them or not. This was to be challenged by later developments such as the Madhyamaka and Yogācāra philosophical schools. It is possible that it was felt that describing the way things truly are by ascribing intrinsic nature to the *dharmas* led to further grasping and attachment, and therefore away from the goal of non-attachment and nirvāṇa. Madhyamaka, essentially a philosophical systematization of the ideas set forth in the Mahāyāna *Perfection of Wisdom sūtras*, argues that *dharmas* too lack inherent self or essence (a unique and defining characteristic); they are not ultimate reality, and can be analysed away. They are 'empty' (śūnya) of intrinsic existence; i.e. they too are dependent on causes for their existence and do not exist on their own side. Ultimately, everything, including emptiness itself, is empty, because the way things truly are is dependently originated; they are mental constructs that depend on the mind apprehending them. This does not mean that they do not exist at all, they just do not exist independently, although Mādhyamika philosophers, such as the famous Nāgārjuna (c. 2nd-3rd century ce), were only concerned with showing the absence of inherent existence.

▶ The Yogācāra

Yogācāra, whose major proponent is Asaṅga (c. 310–390), is an attempt to refute what may be perceived as the nihilistic threat represented by the Madhyamaka teaching of emptiness. In the *Saṃdhinirmocana Sūtra*, the Buddha clearly states that something really exists, a continuously changing flow of perceptions that, in our unawakened state, we conceptualize as distinct subjects and objects, which we mistakenly take for real and permanent entities. For awakened beings, or for the very advanced meditator, this flow of perceptions is non-dual – there is no subject, no object, just a flow of sensations arising and dissolving. The flow of perceptions is all there is; experience and the one who experiences are one, all is mind-only (*cittamātra*), therefore the primary existent is the mind itself.

▶ The Tathāgatagarbha (Buddha-nature)

While the Mādhyamika and Yogācāra philosophers are concerned with ontological issues, the former claiming that everything is a conceptual construct and therefore lacks primary existence, and the latter that the non-dual flow of experience is the primary existent out of which we conceptualize *saṃsāra*, another set of texts were concerned with promoting the Mahāyāna as the path on which, ultimately, all sentient beings should engage to achieve full Buddhahood. In the 3rd century CE

Tathāgatagarbha Sūtra, one of the earliest texts to introduce the idea of the Buddha-nature, the Buddha proclaims that all beings possess, no matter how defiled and unworthy, the Buddha-nature (*tathāgatagarbha*), and therefore, all have the inherent potential to become fully realized Buddhas.

▶ East Asian developments

In East Asia, the Tiantai and the Huayan schools were both concerned with reconciling the diverse teachings found in the extensive collection of Indian texts that had been translated into Chinese, and which all claimed to be the word of the Buddha. They established a fivefold classification system that arranged the *sūtras* in five stages of exposition. The two schools differed as to which *sūtra* was the final teaching of the Buddha, with the Tiantai electing the *Lotus Sūtra*, and the Huayan the *Avataṃsaka Sūtra* (*Flower Garland Sutra*). However, they shared a similar philosophical understanding that drew widely from a Yogācāra philosophical approach and that asserted the interpenetration and mind-made nature of all phenomena: each and every thing is contained in everything else and, by consequence, all things possess Buddha-nature (*tathāgatagarbha*), a crucial concept in East Asian Buddhist schools. In fact, it becomes the very doctrinal foundation of the East Asian tradition, although it is conceptualized in a way that was probably not intended by its Indian proponents. In both the Tiantai and the Huayan schools, the Buddha-nature acquires an ontological status as the underlying permanent basis to reality and the original essence possessed by all beings. This understanding is later meshed with Yogācāra ideas on consciousness, especially related to the nature of awakening, so that the Buddha-nature in every sentient being is merely corrupted by the defilements and awakening is the result of eradicating these defilements to reveal the pure Buddha-nature.

▶ Tibetan developments

Like the Chinese, the Tibetans were faced with a diversity of Buddhist texts and philosophical schools. However, their systematization efforts took a different course. In particular, instead of focusing on the *sūtras* like the Chinese who developed indigenous schools based on specific texts, the Tibetans focused on the philosophical treatises. After the 8th century, and the famous Samye debates, during which the (mostly Chinese) concept of a sudden path to awakening was rejected in favour of a gradual path, they adopted what they usually identified as a Madhyamaka approach, and each school built their entire philosophical understanding of Buddhism, with their (often different) understanding of Madhyamaka at the pinnacle, focusing on developing *bodhicitta*, the mind of awakening, and engaging on the Bodhisattva path.

Global Buddhism

▶ Bodhgayā: a multi-national site of pilgrimage

Ning, Haruki, Jin Yen and Robert are all at Bodhgayā,[43] the place where, in the Buddhist tradition, the Buddha attained awakening. While pilgrimages are not considered an essential practice of Buddhism, they have nonetheless been part of the religious repertoire since its beginning (see Chapter 7), and Buddhists from all traditions make pilgrimages to sites related to the life of the Buddha and other Buddhist saints. Bodhgayā, located in Bihar, northeast India, has a long history of pilgrimage due to its significance both in the life of the Buddha and in Buddhist doctrine, as it marks the culmination of the Buddha's search and the goal of Buddhist practice. As attested in the accounts of the Chinese pilgrims Faxian (337-422) and Xuanzang (602-664), it has been an important site of pilgrimage for Buddhists from Asia and, since its restoration in the 19th century, from all over the world. The main focus of the site is the impressive Bodhi tree, taken to be a direct descendant of the original *Ficus Religiosa* under which the Buddha attained awakening. As they walk around it, the pilgrims pay respect with their hands touching one of the branches above their heads, and their forehead briefly resting against its rough bark. They then place offerings of flowers on the Vajrāsana, a stone platform reputedly built by the Indian emperor Aśoka in the 3rd century BCE to mark the place where the Buddha sat under the tree. To the east of the Bodhi tree, the Mahābodhi Temple stands, a 19th century reconstruction

▲ Figure 9.1 Mahābodhi Temple, Bodhgayā, India

of a 5th century original, although the tradition holds that the first Mahābodhi Temple was also built under Emperor Aśoka in the 3rd century BCE. In the temple, in the position of 'calling the earth to witness' (*bhūmisparśa-mudrā*), sits a Buddha image from the Pāla period (8th–12th century), its original black stone gilded by devotees in recent decades. As the four pilgrims make their way through the sacred complex, they admire the innumerable stupas adorned with offerings and small Buddha images. Despite the multitude and variety of pilgrims – Tibetan monks engaged in full body prostrations, Taiwanese nuns chanting, Thai families circumambulating the temple – the Mahābodhi complex radiates calm and peace that touch everyone who enters it, and even the various beggars and peddlers hawk their wares in subdued tones.

The ancient buildings on the site are surrounded by over 20 temples and monasteries built in the last two centuries by most Buddhist traditions, highlighting their respective regional styles and showcasing, in its birthplace, the diverse and prolific ways in which Buddhism has developed over time and across regions. The site has been under the management of a committee established by the Indian government in 1949, and has also been at the centre of some controversies in the past few decades related to mismanagement, religious sectarianism, loss of artefacts, environmental degradation and poor infrastructure. Despite its recognition in 2002 as a World Heritage Site by UNESCO and the establishment of a new management committee in 2007, it is still unclear whether the site will continue its commercialization and haphazard development, or whether an integrated, collaborative and sustainable programme will be set in place to pursue its development as a pilgrimage and touristic site while safeguarding its religious and sacred character.

Buddhism in the West

The West first became seriously interested in Buddhism in the mid-19th century when a number of Mahāyāna sūtras were translated (such as the *Lotus Sūtra* by Eugène Burnouf, 1801-1852), or adapted (such as the *Lalitavistara* in his poem *The Light of Asia* by Sir Edwin Arnold, 1832-1904). Reception of Buddhist ideas was conflicted: some, like Schopenhauer, saw in it a philosophy of nihilism, and others like Arnold, inspired by the Romantic Movement, hailed it as the ancient wisdom of Asia that would rescue a spiritually moribund Europe. Later scholars, such as England's Thomas Rhys Davids (1843-1922), and his wife, Caroline A. F. Rhys Davids (1857-1942), focused on the translation and study of Pāli texts, the texts of Theravāda Buddhism, and described Buddhism as a rational, ethical and empirical psychology. This interpretation of Buddhism as a 'science of the mind' aimed at self-improvement was adopted by a wide range of supporters in North America and Europe, and promoted in such organizations as the Theosophical Society, founded in 1875 in New York, and soon expanded to Europe, by the American Henry Steel Olcott (1832-1907) and the Russian Helena Blavatsky (1831-1891). The intellectual exploration of Buddhist ideas was not sufficient for some, such as Irish U Dhammaloka (1856-1914) and German Nyānatiloka (1878-1957), who, at the turn of the century, decided to put in practice the teachings of the Buddha and were ordained as monks in Burma.

After the Second World War, interest in Buddhism picked up again, especially Zen Buddhism in the US in the 1950s and 1960s, with the Beat Generation, and Tibetan Buddhism in Europe, in the late 1960s and 1970s. Westerners travelled to Asia, and Asian teachers travelled to North America and Europe. A multitude of centres, temples, monasteries and other groups linked to Asian traditions, as well as Western adaptations, were established at a fast rate. This was accompanied by an influx of immigrants from Southeast Asia after the Vietnam War (1959–75) who established Theravāda temples in many European countries and in North America where Japanese and Chinese Buddhists had already been present since the mid-19th century.

The complexion of Buddhism in the West in the 21st century is therefore very diverse and plural, and scholarly attempts to organize it into categories have met with controversy, especially when drawing boundaries along ethnic and cultural lines, such as Charles Prebisch's well-known description of North American 'two Buddhisms'. Recently, Martin Baumann has highlighted four broad categories of Buddhists in Europe based on immigration and convert status and attitudes towards traditions.[44] First-generation conservative immigrants thus appear more similar to convert Buddhists who follow Asian traditions closely, than to second-generation immigrants who challenge the traditions and are, in that respect, more similar to convert Buddhists who are striving to develop forms of Buddhism adapted to the modern West. However, Paul Numrich points out that research in North America shows a phenomenon of 'parallel congregations',[45] in which separation along ethnic lines is prevalent within institutions that cater both for immigrant and convert groups under the same roof, but at different times and in different ways. For example, a Theravāda Buddhist temple may offer meditation and Dharma classes to converts, and follow the traditional calendar of *pujas* for the immigrant population performed in the immigrants' native tongue.

▶ Buddhism on the world stage

These divisions, to a certain extent, are reflections of the varied and sometimes conflicting interests and agendas of Buddhist communities around the world that find themselves interacting not only, as described above, in Bodhgayā, but also on the global stage, and in diverse national settings, especially those where Buddhism is a relative newcomer to the religious marketplace. Buddhism is not new to changes and adaptations, and experienced many as it travelled throughout Asia and adapted to local cultures and different worldviews. Like all religions that have to deal with the age of consumption, ever-faster communication and globalization, it has been undergoing yet another transformation and, despite the plurality and diversity of its traditions, it is possible to discern the emergence of a 'global' Buddhist movement, which recognizes a shared identity and common goals. This global movement is not monolithic, and it may be best understood as convergences of interest around the pursuit of certain objectives. These convergences display at least three common characteristics that make them recognizably part of this global movement:

▶ They bring together a wide range of representatives from many Buddhist traditions, charismatic leaders, scholars and scholar-practitioners.

▶ They seek to articulate forms of Buddhism that are relevant in conditions of 21st-century modernity while appreciating the value and importance of traditional structures and practices.

▶ They recognize a shared identity above sectarian differences and promote an ecumenical approach.

Many areas illustrate these characteristics and exemplify how the global Buddhist movement coalesces around specific issues, such as socially engaged Buddhism, Buddhism and science, and advocacy for the full ordination of women.

▶ The path to re-establishing full ordination for women

The advocacy movement to re-establish full ordination lineages for women in the Theravāda and Tibetan traditions is a good illustration of global Buddhism, as it brings together practitioners, scholars, scholar-practitioners, influential leaders such as the Dalai Lama, and draws on a modernist discourse that promotes women's equal rights, but still attempts to do so within the framework of established traditions. The movement also works across traditions and draws together Theravāda, Tibetan, Chinese and Western Buddhists.

In Chapter 3, we saw that the only extant lineage of nuns is the *Dharmagupta* established in China. In Sri Lanka, Thailand, Burma and in Tibetan Buddhism, orders of female renouncers have attracted women who wanted to live the monastic life. However, women joining these groups cannot obtain full ordination because this can only be conferred with ordination ceremonies that include a specified number of monks and nuns. Since the female Theravādin and the Tibetan ordination lineages (the latter is called Mūlasarvāstivāda) are no longer extant, nuns can no longer be ordained in these traditions. The status of these female monastics is much lower than that of monks, and they do not benefit from the advantages associated with being a fully ordained member of the *Saṇgha*, such as religious education, government benefits, and financial support from the community. As was discussed in Chapter 3, this has deleterious consequences for women who seek to pursue the monastic life and for lay followers, especially women.

One option to reinstate full ordination for women is for Chinese nuns to participate in the ordination ceremonies, but this has been dismissed by the official monastic institutions as invalid, because the ordination lineage is different. However, some women decided that this was a valid option and ordination ceremonies were held with the help of Chinese Dharmagupta nuns, and monks ordained in the Theravāda lineage, and with strong support from Western Buddhists, both monastic and lay.

In Sri Lanka, where women's full ordination had received lukewarm support from the male monastic establishment, an international ordination took place and restarted a Sri Lanka nun lineage in 1998. In Thailand, Chatsumarn Kabilsingh, a professor at Thammasat University in Bangkok, received full ordination in the Dharmagupta Chinese lineage in 2003 amid great controversy and fierce opposition from the Thai *Saṅgha*. However, more than a decade later, these ordinations in the Theravāda tradition are still contested and not recognized by the monastic authorities and governments of traditional Buddhist countries. This means that these nuns' monastic status is not legally recognized, nor are they entitled to government benefits, such as free transportation, public funding, and government identification cards.

In an event emblematic of global Buddhism gathering senior representatives from most traditions, and well-known academics along with practitioners, and scholar-practitioners, an *International Congress on Buddhist Women's Role in the Saṅgha* was held in 2007 and concluded that:

'the [Tibetan nun full] ordination needs to be restarted, can be restarted, and must be restarted. Otherwise, Buddhism will be looked down upon by modern society as

discriminating against women
and Buddhists will be limiting
their own ability to benefit
society.'[46]

On the last day of the conference, the Dalai Lama issued an unqualified expression of support, which he reiterated several times since.

'After extensive research and
consultation with leading
Vinaya scholars and Saṅgha
members of the Tibetan
tradition and Buddhist
traditions internationally,
and with the backing of the
Tibetan Buddhist community,
since 1960s, I express my full
support for the establishment
of the [nuns' order] in the
Tibetan tradition.'[47]

However, the Dalai Lama's support has not yet translated into concrete results, and full ordination has not yet been fully available for women in the Tibetan tradition – although some women ordain through the Chinese Dharmagupta ordination lineage. At this date, a new research committee has been established by the Dalai Lama to examine the Tibetan Buddhist tradition thoroughly and offer recommendations on the possible avenues for instituting a *bhikṣuni* lineage in the Tibetan tradition. In late 2012, the committee also sought scholarly information from Thubten Chodron and Jampa Tsedroen, two Western nuns in the Tibetan tradition. These nuns are fully ordained in the Dharmagupta lineage, and Jampa Tsedroen (Carola Roloff) is also a scholar at an academic institution in the West (University of Hamburg), highlighting the trend of global Buddhism to mesh Western academic research with traditional practice and scholarship.

Despite its apparent lack of immediate and complete success, the movement to re-establish full ordination for women is representative of global Buddhism. It brings together a wide range of Buddhist traditions and interested parties to pursue a goal that is clearly informed by modern ideals of women's rights, but it does so while seeking to remain within the framework of the relevant traditions, yet acknowledging the non-sectarian dimension of the goal. Similar traits can be found in the work of such organizations as the Buddhist Peace Fellowship,[48] which focuses on peace, social justice, and environmental sustainability; and the Mind & Life Institute which, according to its website, seeks to 'build a scientific understanding of the mind to reduce suffering and promote well-being'.[49]

▶ Future opportunities and challenges

It is my hope that this brief introduction has succeeded in illustrating the diversity and splendour of Buddhist traditions historically and in the present time, and in giving a taste of their richness and dynamism. Buddhism, like other religious traditions, is on the cusp of many changes as the world moves deeper into the 21st century. Possibly unlike some of these traditions, Buddhism may be constitutionally well equipped to face the challenges of modernity because its fundamental description of the nature of reality is based on concepts of change and impermanence. Buddhist ideas have shown resilience and great capacity for adaptation while retaining essential characteristics as they were integrated and combined with indigenous systems of thought over 25 centuries of history. At the local and global levels, many Buddhists seem willing to engage fully with modernity and the challenges of the 21st century: local Buddhist communities in Asia and the West have become involved with social issues, disaster responses and environmental concerns, and they have also come together to pursue these efforts globally.

On a less positive note, Buddhist ideals have also been invoked for nationalistic, racist and discriminatory purposes, which are hallmarks of fundamentalist reactions to modernity showing that Buddhism has not been spared exploitation by reactionary-minded individuals and groups. How the wider Buddhist community reacts to these will be a measure of its strength and cohesion.

Certain current trends, related to globalization, have been decried as representing a risk to the authenticity of Buddhism or as constructive adaptations. These include the growing uniformization of teachings and practices that threatens to obliterate cultural diversity, the instrumentalization of Buddhist teachings and practices for worldly goals, and the dilution of its ethical principles and ascetic practices that produces a watered down commercialized version of Buddhism. Some have suggested that the integration of Buddhist principles in the wider global society is to be applauded, but others warn that, through such process of integration and secularization, the significance of the Buddha's message of ultimate liberation and transcendence is being lost.

The Five Precepts

These are the precepts customarily taken by lay Buddhists. They are particularly followed on observance and festival days, as Ning did in Chapters 1 and 5.

1   Refrain from harming sentient beings: this applies to all sentient beings as we are all part of *saṃsāra*.

2   Refrain from taking what is not given: this goes further than not stealing as it implies a conscious reflection on what is truly given.

3   Refrain from wrong speech: this includes every kind of speech that may be hurtful or even just futile, including gossip and spreading rumours.

4   Refrain from sexual misconduct: this is not limited to sexual actions, but more broadly to indulgences in the senses.

5   Refrain from intoxicants: this is not an outright ban, as in Islam for example, but rather intoxicants such as alcohol and mind-altering drugs should be avoided because they may lead to breaking the other precepts as awareness is compromised.

The Ten Perfections (*pāramitā/ pāramī*)

The perfections are qualities perfected by the Bodhisattva (Pāli: Bodhisatta) as he advances on the path to Buddhahood in the Theravāda tradition.

6   Generosity: the practice of generosity through which the Bodhisatta gives to all beings regardless of their worthiness.

7   Morality: the practice of good conduct (epitomized by the Five Precepts).

8   Renunciation: the practice of renouncing worldly possessions.

9   Diligence: the constant efforts made by the Bodhisatta to help all beings.

10 Wisdom: the practice of distinguishing between wholesome and unwholesome behaviours and attitudes in order to help all beings.

11 Patience: the practice of bearing with calm the unwholesome behaviours and attitudes of others.

12 Truthfulness: the practice through which the Bodhisatta keeps his word in all circumstances.

13 Determination: the Bodhisatta never gives up his activities for the welfare of all beings.

14 Loving kindness: the attitude of deep care that the Bodhisatta brings to his efforts to achieve the welfare of all beings.

15 Equanimity: the Bodhisatta welcomes all results of his efforts with detachment and no expectation to receive anything in return for his efforts.

Five Objects

Five objects that are part of the monastic life or associated with Buddhist rituals and practices.

16 The begging bowl is one of the eight requisites – the material possessions that monks and nuns were originally allowed in the Vinaya. The begging bowl should not be made of precious material, and should be used until it is no longer functional. While monks no longer eat out of their begging bowl, they still carry it to receive alms when they go on alms-rounds in Theravāda countries.

17 The three robes are also part of the few material possessions allowed to monks and nuns, and they have undergone many changes as Buddhism travelled through Asia, from changes of colour (saffron, or brownish, in Sri Lanka and Southeast Asia, to maroon in Tibet, to grey and black in East Asian Buddhism) to changes of shape (three lengths of cloth are allowed in Theravāda Buddhism, but Tibetan and East Asian monks and nuns wear sewn garments).

18 The *mala* is a rosary that is used to count recitations of a prayer, a mantra or prostrations. They usually have 108 beads and can be made of a wide range of material, including human bones.

19 The bell is used in most Buddhist traditions to mark time during the day, during ceremonies and rituals. Bells vary in shape and size from hand-held bells used in Tibetan pujas to gigantic bells in Chinese temples. Beyond their pragmatic use for marking time, they have ritual and merit-making purposes.

20 The *vajra* (Tibetan: *dorje*) is an object representing the diamond thunderbolt used in Tibetan Buddhist rituals along with a bell. It symbolizes the awakening experience and also skilful means, while the bell symbolizes wisdom.

Ten Practices for Every Day

These practices are not necessarily Buddhist although they are based on Buddhist practices. They can be seen as 'developing wholesome attitudes' practices or as 'developing faith' practices, whichever is most appealing to those who undertake them.

21 Develop compassionate love for yourself and others: think of yourself as being a small child, or a small animal, or any being that elicits a warm and caring feeling from you. Now think of yourself as you are, and extend a warm and caring feeling to yourself. Now extend the warm and caring feeling to people you care for. Finally, when you feel comfortable with extending this feeling to people you already care for, extend it to people you feel indifferent to, then to people you find irritating, and finally to all beings.

22 Develop mindfulness of the body: what are you doing now? How is your body positioned? Do you have any stress, pressure, pain, or discomfort in any part of your body? In what way are you breathing (slow, rapid, deep, shallow)? What are your surroundings like? Just focus on the physical sensations of your body and the environment around you, without judging them, and simply noting them.

23 Develop mindfulness of the mind: what are you thinking now? What kind of emotions are your thoughts stirring? Are your thoughts slow or rapid? Are they scattered or cohesive? Just examine your thoughts as if you were watching a film, without judging them, and simply noting them.

24 Develop gratitude: reflect on all the good things in your life, whether it is material things such as a place to live, food to eat, and clothes to wear, or relationships, family, friends and colleagues. Make a list on a daily basis for all the things we often take for granted such as health, material comfort, friends and family, and feel gratitude for these. Even in the bleakest of circumstances, one can find something to feel gratitude for.

25 Develop mindful generosity: choose a charity or a cause to give to on a regular basis. Choose it because you take an interest in its work, then follow what it does. Base your giving on what you think is important to contribute to.

26 Develop active kindness: try to do a good deed a day. Whether it is helping someone with a pushchair go up the stairs, or give your seat in the bus, or doing the shopping for a busy friend or relative, do something helpful for someone else without expecting anything in return.

27 Develop a sense of interdependence: when you use something, or eat something, think of all the work that has gone into the product you are consuming, of all the people that have been involved in its production, its transport, and its packaging. Reflect on how everything we usually take for granted is someone's labour without which our life would be much more difficult.

28 Accept change: think about how change is unavoidable but necessary for life. Change is when a baby transforms into a child and into an adult, when a seed becomes a shoot and then a tree. Change is the stuff of life.

29 Accept impermanence: because everything changes, nothing is permanent. Practices such as mindfulness meditation focus on developing an awareness of impermanence in our bodily and mental processes.

Our bodily sensations, our emotions, our feelings all rise and fade away, just like the breath. Recognize that this is the nature of life from individual cells to sentient beings to galaxies.

30 Develop *anatta*: *anatta* (Skt: *anātman*) is the concept that no self can be identified. Self here is understood as an unchanging, permanent entity that is truly me. Try to pinpoint what is really 'you' in a stable, enduring way. Is it the body? Think about how your body has evolved since you were born. Is it some personality trait? Think about how you have changed since you were a child, a teenager or a young adult. Is it your emotions or feelings? Remember how these fluctuate even in the course of one day. This is particularly useful when experiencing negative emotions or feelings, as it allows to realize that we are not our emotions, our compulsions, our habits or our failures.

Five Classical Buddhist Works

31 *The Suttanipāta*: a book from the Pāli canon that contains short *suttas*. It is not as well known as the *Dhammapada*, but nonetheless equally worth reading. A scholarly translation is K. R. Norman's *The Group of Discourses* (Pāli Text Society, 2001).

32 *The Therīgathā*: another book from the same section of the Pāli canon that contains the verses of the female elders (*therī*) upon attaining awakening. A testament to the egalitarian attitude found in early Buddhism. A scholarly translation is K. R.'s Norman's *Elders' Verses II* (*Therīgāthā*) (Pāli Text Society, 2007).

33 *The Bodhicaryāvatāra of Śantideva* sets out the path of the Mahāyāna Bodhisattva in striking and evocative verses. There are a multitude of translations and commentaries by ancient and contemporary masters, including His Holiness the Dalai Lama. A scholarly translation is Kate Crosby and Andrew Skilton's *Bodhicaryāvatāra* (Oxford University Press, 2008). The introduction by Professor Paul Williams provides a succinct and very informative overview of Mahāyāna thought.

34 *The Life of Milarepa* by Tsangnyon Heruka tells the life of the great Tibetan ascetic Milarepa. A scholarly translation is Andrew Quintman's *The Life of Milarepa* (Penguin Classics, 2010) with a useful introduction by Professor Donald Lopez.

35 *Eihei Shingi* by Dōgen introduces us to the thought of the great Zen master through the seemingly mundane perspective of instructions to the cook, exemplifying the spirit of Zen and giving an insight of the day-to-day life of the monk. A scholarly translation is Taigen Daniel Leighton and Shohaku Okumura's *Dōgen's Pure Standards for the Zen Community* (State University of New York Press, 1995). The introduction is also very helpful.

Five Contemporary Buddhist Works

36 Chogye Trichen Rinpoche, *Parting from the Four Attachments* (Snow Lion, 2003): a commentary by a 20th century Tibetan Sakya master of a core teaching of Tibetan Buddhism. Chogye Trichen Rinpoche adapts the teachings to a Western audience, while retaining the traditional approach and understanding.

37 Sylvia Boorstein, *Don't Just Do Something, Sit There: A Mindfulness Retreat with Sylvia Boorstein* (HarperOne, 1996): a guide to setting up your own mindfulness meditation retreat at home. It emphasizes, with a delightful sense of humour, that the point of mindfulness meditation is to develop mindfulness in all aspects of one's life at all times.

38 Master Sheng Yen, *Living in the 21st Century: A Buddhist View* (Sheng Yen Foundation, 2011): a short guide to apply Buddhist ethics to contemporary life from the perspective of the Taiwanese Chan Master. It deals with such areas as the environment, spiritual life and dealing with daily life issues.

39 Thubten Chodron, *Taming the Monkey Mind* (Heian International, 1999): a Western Tibetan nun writes about Tibetan Buddhism from a contemporary perspective.

40 Mary Evelyn Tucker and Duncan Ryuken Williams (eds.), *Buddhism and Ecology: The Interconnection of Dharma and Deeds* (Harvard University Press, 1998): a collection of essays on the application of Buddhist ideas to environmental issues, including many essays by scholar-practitioners from several Buddhist traditions.

Five Scholarly Books on Buddhism

41 David Snellgrove, *Indo-Tibetan Buddhism: Indian Buddhists and their Tibetan Successors* (Serindia, 1987): a classic study of Indo-Tibetan Buddhism.

42 Peter Harvey, *An Introduction to Buddhist Ethics: Foundations, Values and Issues* (Cambridge University Press, 2000): a comprehensive examination of ethics from a Buddhist perspective, written with precision and depth.

43 John Kieschnick, *The Impact of Buddhism on Chinese Material Culture* (Princeton University Press, 2003): a fascinating account of Buddhism in China told through the impact on its material culture.

44 David McMahan (ed.), *Buddhism in the Modern World* (Routledge, 2012): a collection of essays that addresses the different faces of Buddhism in Asia and in the West, and a variety of issues such as politics, gender and social engagement.

45 Ellison Banks Findly (ed.), *Women's Buddhism, Buddhism's Women: Tradition, Revision, Renewal* (Wisdom Publications, 2000): essays on women in many Buddhist traditions from a historical and contemporary perspective.

Ten Buddhist Festivals

46 February: Makha Puja (Thailand)/Navam Full Moon Poya Day (Sri Lanka) commemorates the Buddha's teaching of the monastic rules.

47 February: Monlam Prayer Festival (Tibetan) started as a Gelug tradition in the early 15th century, but is now celebrated by all Tibetans.

48 April: Songkran (Thailand)/Aluth Avurudu (Sri Lanka) celebrates the Buddhist New Year.

49 May: Visakha Puja (Thailand)/Vesak (Sri Lanka) commemorates the Buddha's birth, awakening and entering into final nirvāṇa.

50 July: Asalha Puja (Thailand)/Esala (Sri Lanka) commemorates the Buddha's First Turning of the Wheel of Dhamma, the first sermon he gave after his awakening. It also marks the beginning of the rainy season retreat during which, in the canonical texts, monks stayed in residence in a monastery.

51 July 6: His Holiness the 14th Dalai Lama's Birthday, an occasion celebrated by Tibetans and in Tibetan

Buddhist centres across the world, especially by offering Long-Life Pujas to His Holiness.

52 October: Pavarana **(Thailand)**/Vap Full Moon Poya Day (Sri Lanka), the end of the rainy season retreat.

53 November: Katina **(Thailand)**/Cheevara Puja **(Sri Lanka)**; during the month following the end of the rainy season retreat, the laity makes an offering of new robes (and other necessities) to the saṅgha.

54 Saka Dawa (Tibetan) is the Tibetan celebration of the Buddha's birth, awakening and entering into final nirvāṇa. It is held during the 15th day of the 4th lunar month.

55 Guanyin (Chinese) celebrates the birthday (19th of 2nd lunar month), awakening (19th of 6th lunar month) and renunciation (19th of 9th lunar month) of the Bodhisattva Guanyin (Skt: Avalokiteśvara) who is worshipped widely in East Asian and Tibetan Buddhism.

Five Global Buddhism Groups

56 Gaia House, Devon, UK, meditation retreat centre, http://gaiahouse.co.uk/

57 Sakyadhita, International Association of Buddhist Women, www.sakyadhita.org

58 Buddhist Peace Fellowship, Socially Engaged Buddhism, founded in the USA, www.buddhistpeacefellowship.org

59 International Network of Engaged Buddhism, Socially Engaged Buddhism, founded in Thailand, www.inebnetwork.org/ineb/home

60 Mind & Life Institute, integrating modern science with Buddhist practices and ideas, www.mindandlife.org

Five Feature Films

61 *The Cup* by Khyentse Norbu (1999). The riveting (and often comic) adventures of young Tibetan monks who scheme to watch the 1998 Football World Cup final game despite the older monks' veto.

62 *Enlightenment Guaranteed* by Doris Dörrie (1999). The quest of two German brothers in Japan develops in unexpected ways as they struggle with culture shock.

63 *The Silent Holy Stones* by Pema Tseden (2004). The moving story of a young monk and a Tibetan *tulku* (recognized reincarnation) as they try to integrate the novelty of television and the strict regime of monastic training.

64 *Un Budha* by Diego Rafecas (2005). A take on contemporary Buddhism in Latin America with the story of two brothers who face each other during a retreat at a Zen centre.

65 *Zen* by Banmei Takahashi (2009). The life of Sōtō Zen founder Dogen in 13th century Japan told as an epic legend with beautiful landscapes and an attention to authentic details.

Five Documentaries

66 *My Reincarnation* by Jennifer Fox (2010). A documentary on the life of Tibetan Buddhist Master Chögyal Namkhai Norbu depicting him in an extraordinarily frank and open light as he teaches Western students and deals with his son.

67 *Amongst White Clouds* by Edward Burger (2006). A rare glimpse of Chinese Buddhist hermits living in the Zhongnan Mountain range of Northwest China.

68 *Souls of Zen – Buddhism, Ancestors, and the 2011 Tsunami in Japan* by Tim Graf and Jakob Montrasio (2012). This documentary explores the Buddhist reaction to the 2011 Tsunami in Japan, and especially how the Buddhist clergy addresses its religious, psychological and ritual challenges in the most affected region.

69 *Blessings: The Tsoknyi Nangchen Nuns of Tibet* by Victress Hitchcock (2009). This is the story of the encounter between the Western followers of Tsoknyi Rinpoche and Tibetan nuns who have been rebuilding their monasteries after the destruction caused by the Cultural Revolution.

70 *Buddha's Lost Children* by Mark Verkerk (2006). This documentary describes an unusual Thai monk, a former boxer, who has built an orphanage, a school and a clinic for children in the impoverished and troubled region of the Northern Thai-Burmese border.

Ten Places to Visit

71 *India: Bodh Gaya,* the place where the Buddha attained awakening, and a common site of pilgrimage for all Buddhist traditions.

72 *Sri Lanka: Anuradhapura*, the ancient site of the Mahāvihāra (the Great Monastery) that was established in the 3rd century BCE, and played a major role in the transmission of Theravāda Buddhism.

73 *Cambodia: the Angkor Wat Temple* complex dates from the 12th century Khmer Empire and is one of the most fascinating sites of Hindu/Buddhist history in Southeast Asia.

74 *Thailand: the Sukhothai Historical Park* is located some distance away from the myriads of tourists that invade Bangkok and Ayutthaya. The historical park is refreshing and showcases the ancient capital of Siam built in the 13th century. Its iconographic style is well known for its flowing elegance.

75 *Indonesia: the Borobudur Temple* complex was built between the 8th and 9th century in Central Java and attests to the Buddhist heritage of the island.

76 *China: the Lingyin Temple* dates from the 4th century, and was one of the most important in Chinese Chan Buddhism.

77 *Tibet: the Potala Palace* (former residence of the Dalai Lamas) and the Jokhang monastery are two of the religious sites that survived the Cultural Revolution almost intact in Lhasa, Tibet's capital. Both are central sites of Tibetan Buddhism.

78 *Japan: Nara and Kyoto* are two inescapable cities to visit for anyone interested in Buddhism. The ancient imperial capital of Nara was built in the 8th century when the Japanese empire was a strong supporter of Buddhism, and Kyoto's ancient temples and gardens exemplify Zen's relationship with nature.

79 *Burma: the Pagan Archaeological Zone* is the site of the ancient capital of the Burmese Kingdom of Pagan (9th-13th century), and boasts over 200 temples and stupas that remained from the many thousands that were built during the Pagan Empire.

80 *Nepal: the Svayambhunath and Bodhnath stupas* in Kathmandu, two ancient holy sites whose origins are lost in myth. The Bodhnath stupa is said to contain relics from the Buddha who preceded Śākyamuni. It is a focus of worship for the Tibetan Buddhists who live in Nepal.

Ten Buddhist Groups in the UK

81 Amaravati Monastery: **Therāvada Thai Forest Tradition**

82 The Samatha Trust: **Therāvada Calm Meditation**

83 Vipassana Meditation Center: **Therāvada Insight Meditation, Goenka**

84 Community of Interbeing UK: **Thich Nhat Hanh, Mahāyāna Zen Buddhism**

85 Western Chan Fellowship: **Chinese Buddhism, Zen Buddhism**

86 Kagyu Samye Ling: **Tibetan Kagyu-pa, Trungpa Rinpoche**

87 Foundation for the Preservation of the Mahayana Tradition: **Tibetan Gelug-pa**

88 Rigpa UK: **Tibetan Nyingmapa, Sogyal Rinpoche**

89 Soka Gakkai International UK: **Nichiren Japanese Buddhism**

90 Triratna Buddhist Community (formerly Friends of the Western Buddhist Order): **Western Buddhism, Sangharakshita**

Ten Websites

There are countless Internet sources on Buddhism varying in depth and quality. These are a good and reliable place to start exploring Buddhism online.

91 Buddhanet: **wide range of Buddhism-related resources, www.buddhanet.net/**

92 Quiet Mountain: resources on Tibetan Buddhism, www.quietmountain.org/buddhism.htm

93 Access to Insight: readings and resources on Theravāda Buddhism, www.accesstoinsight.org

94 Vipassana Fellowship: online insight meditation courses, www.vipassana.com/

95 Network of Buddhist Women in Europe: a resource for Buddhist women in Europe, www.buddhistwomen.eu/EN/index.php/Main/HomePage

96 Thai Bhikkhuni: Venerable Dhammananda, the first fully ordained Theravāda nun in Thailand, www.thaibhikkhunis.org/eng/index.php?option=com_frontpage&Itemid=1

97 Buddhist Channel: Buddhist news online: www.buddhistchannel.tv/

98 American Buddhist Perspective: a young scholar-practitioner discusses topical issues from a scholarly and practice-minded perspective, www.patheos.com/blogs/americanbuddhist/

99 My Buddha is Pink: a personal blog about being gay, Buddhist and how the two interact, http://mybuddhaispink.blogspot.com/

100 Buddhist Geeks: online Buddhist community, www.buddhistgeeks.com

Notes

1 From www.wnrf.org/cms/statuswr.shtml [last accessed 16 September 2013].

2 From http://thedhamma.com/buddhists_in_the_world.htm [last accessed 16 September 2013].

3 From https://www.cia.gov/library/publications/the-world-factbook/geos/xx.html#People (6.77% of a 7 billion world population; data accessed 27 June 2013).

4 Rupert Gethin, *The Foundations of Buddhism* (Oxford University Press, 1998: p. 167).

5 United Nations Resolution 54/115. Available at: www.un.org/ga/search/view_doc.asp?symbol=A/RES/54/115 [last accessed 16 September 2013].

6 Lance S. Cousins 'The Dating of the Historical Buddha: A Review Article'. *Journal of the Royal Asiatic Society*, Series 3, 6.1 (1996): 57–63.

7 John Strong, The Buddha, A Short Biography (OneWorld, 2001): especially pp. 12–3; for the story of the Buddha in Pāli canonical texts, see N. A. Jayawickrama (translator), *The Story of Gotama Buddha* (Pali Text Society, 2002); also the Mahāpadāna Sutta in Maurice Walshe (translator), *The Long Discourses of the Buddha: A Translation of the Dīgha Nikāya* (Wisdom Publications, 1987).

8 Rupert Gethin, *The Foundations of Buddhism* (Oxford University Press, 1998): pp. 16–27.

9 Paul Williams, *Buddhist Thought: A Complete Introduction to the Indian Tradition* (Routledge, 2000).

10 James W. Coleman, 'The New Buddhism: some empirical findings' in Christopher Queen and Duncan R. Williams (ed.) *American Buddhism: Methods and Findings in Recent Scholarship* (Routledge, 1999): pp. 94–5.

11 Peter Harvey, *An Introduction to Buddhism* (Cambridge University Press, 1990): pp. 179–180.

12 Life of Zen available online at http://global.sotozennet.or.jp/ eng/photos_videos/life_of_Zen/eng/movie_player_eng.html

13 Monica Lindberg Falk, *Making Fields of Merit: Buddhist Female Ascetics and Gendered Orders in Thailand* (NIAS Press, 2007); especially chapter 3.

14 Thomas Fuller, 'Extremism rises among Myanmar Buddhists', *New York Times*, 20 June 2013.

15 Also see Ian Harris (ed.), *Buddhism and Politics in Twentieth Century Asia* (Continuum International Publishing, 2010).

16 Nihonshoki scroll 19 'Transmission of Buddhism to Japan'. Available at: http://nihonshoki.wikidot.com/scroll-19-kimmei [last accessed 16 September 2013].

17 John S. Bowman, *Columbia Chronologies of Asian History and Culture* (Columbia University Press, 2000)

18 Norimitsu Onishi, 'In Japan, Buddhism may be dying out', *New York Times*, 14 July 2008.

19 For the disappearance of nuns in ancient India, see Nancy Auer Falk, 'The case of the vanishing nuns: the fruits of ambivalence in ancient Indian Buddhism', in Nancy Auer Falk and Rita M. Gross (eds), *Unspoken Worlds: Women's Religious Lives in Non-Western Cultures* (Harper & Row Publishers, 1980); and Ellison Banks Findly, 'Women and the Arahant issue in early P̄ali literature', *Journal of Feminist Studies in Religion*, 15.01, 2006, pp. 57–60.

20 See also 'An International Congress on Buddhist Women's Role in the Sangha, held in 2007': see the summary report, including excellent historical background online at http:// www.berzinarchives.com/web/en/archives/approaching_ buddhism/world_today/summary_report_2007

21 For the impact of nuns' absence on the laity, see, for example, Susanne Mrozik, 'In the company of spiritual friends: Sri Lanka's Buddhist nuns'. Available at: www.bhikkhuni.net/wp-

content/uploads/2013/07/sri-lankas-buddhist-nuns1.pdf [last accessed 16 September 2013].

22 'Outstanding Women in World Buddhism', online at http://www. buddhanet.net/elearning/history/women_world.htm

23 Joan Halifax Roshi's biographical information, available at: www.upaya.org/roshi/ [last accessed 16 September 2013] See also, Joan Halifax, *Being With Dying: Cultivating Compassion and Fearlessness in the Presence of Death* (Shambhala Publications: 2009); and Kristin Barendsen, 'Joan Halifax: Fearless and Fragile' in Shambhala Sun, May 2009, available online at http://www.shambhalasun.com/index.php? option=content&task=view&id=3361.

24 'Lesbian couple wed in a Buddhist ceremony in Taiwan', 13 August 2012. Available at: www.fridae. asia/newsfeatures/2012/08/13/11854.lesbian-couple-wed-in-a-buddhist-ceremony-in-taiwan [last accessed 16 September 2013]

25 Her Eminence Mindrolling Jetsün Khandro Rinpoche's biography, online at http://mjkr.org/biography.cfm79 'About Connecting with a Teacher', FPMT Mandala, online at http:// www.mandalamagazine.org/archives/mandala-issues-for-2007/october/aboutconnecting-with-a-teacher/ [last accessed 16 September 2013]

26 'About Connecting with a Teacher', FPMT Mandala. Available at: www.mandalamagazine.org/archives/mandala-issues-for-2007/october/about-connecting-with-a-teacher/ [last accessed 16 September 2013]

27 Paul Williams, *Buddhist Thought: A Complete Introduction to the Indian Tradition* (Routledge, 2000): p. 46.

28 For scholars who argue that answers to the question concerning the Buddha after death are not useful, see in particular Steven Collins, *Selfless Persons: Imagery and Thought in Theravada Buddhism* (Cambridge University Press, 1982); pp. 135–8.

29 Based on Rupert Gethin, *The Foundations of Buddhism* (Oxford University Press, 1998): p. 81.

30 José Cabezón, 'On the Ethics of the Tibetan Self-Immolations Religious Dispatches, 16 June 2013. Accessible online at http://www.religiondispatches.org/archive/politics/7126/on_the_ethics_of_the_tibetan_self_immolations_/

31 For popular books about Western psychology and forming habits see, for example, Jeremy Dean, *Making Habits, Breaking Habits: Why We Do Things, Why We Don't, and How to Make Any Change Stick* (Da Capo Lifelong Books, 2013).

32 Lara Villadiego and Biel Calderon, 'In pictures: Thailand's female monks', Aljazeera, 17 June 2013. Available at: www.aljazeera.com/indepth/inpictures/2013/06/20136295128230163.html [last accessed 16 September 2013]

33 Patrice Ladwig and Gregory Kourilsky, *Caring for the beyond: Two Lao Buddhist festivals for the deceased* (Lao Art Media Production, Vientiane 2007).

34 www.karuna-institute.co.uk/

35 www.umassmed.edu/cfm

36 www.stanford.edu/group/ccare/cgi-bin/wordpress/

37 www.mindandlife.org

38 Megan Rose Dickey, 'Facebook Is Injecting Buddhism Into Its Core Business So It Can Be More Compassionate', *Business Insider*, 25 June 2013. Available at: www.businessinsider.com/facebook-injects-buddhism-into-business-2013-6 [last accessed 16 September 2013]

39 Thich Nath Hanh's visit to Google: www.youtube.com/watch?feature=player_embedded&v=7Pd5NdgOoJA [last accessed 16 September 2013].

40 Jon Kabat-Zinn's visit to Google: www.youtube.com/watch?v=3nwwKbM_vJc [last accessed 16 September 2013].

41 Paul Williams, *Mahāyāna Buddhism: The Doctrinal Foundations* 2nd ed. (Routledge, 2009); see especially the introduction

42 Williams, 2000, p. 67; see also Gethin, 1998, pp. 141-2, and the *Mahānidānasutta* D. II. 68; for the formula reversing this cycle of suffering, see the *Bahudhātukasutta* M. III. 63-64.

43 For further information on Bodh Gayā, see the official website: www.mahabodhi.com/

44 Martin Baumann, 'Modernist Interpretations of Buddhism in Europe', in David McMahan (ed.), *Buddhism in the Modern World* (Routledge, 2012), p. 127.

45 P. D. Numrich, 'Two Buddhisms further reconsidered', *Contemporary Buddhism*, Vol. 4. No. 1, May 2003.

46 'An International Congress on Buddhist Women's Role in the Sangha, held in 2007': see the summary report, including excellent historical background online at www.berzinarchives. com/web/en/archives/approaching_buddhism/world_today/ summary_report_2007_international_c/part_1.html [last accessed 16 September 2013]

47 Statement made by HHDL, International Congress on Buddhist Women's Role in the Sangha, 18-20 July 2007.

48 www.buddhistpeacefellowship.org

49 www.mindandlife.org

Other resources

Books

John S. Bowman, *Columbia Chronologies of Asian History and Culture* (Columbia University Press, 2000).

James W. Coleman, 'The New Buddhism: some empirical findings', in Christopher Queen and Duncan R. Williams (ed.) *American Buddhism: Methods and Findings in Recent Scholarship* (Routledge, 1999).

Lance S. Cousins, 'The Dating of the Historical Buddha: A Review Article', *Journal of the Royal Asiatic Society*, Series 3, 6.1 (1996): 57–63.

Rupert Gethin, *The Foundations of Buddhism* (Oxford University Press, 1998).

Joan Halifax, *Being With Dying: Cultivating Compassion and Fearlessness in the Presence of Death* (Shambhala Publications, 2009).

Ian Harris (ed.), *Buddhism and Politics in Twentieth Century Asia* (Continuum International Publishing, 2010).

Peter Harvey, *An Introduction to Buddhism* (Cambridge University Press, 1990).

N. A. Jayawickrama (translator), *The Story of Gotama Buddha* (Pali Text Society, 2002).

Patrice Ladwig and Gregory Kourilsky, *Caring for the Beyond: Two Lao Buddhist Festivals for the Deceased* (Lao Art Media Production, Vientiane 2007).

ALL THAT MATTERS: BUDDHISM

Monica Lindberg Falk, *Making Fields of Merit: Buddhist Female Ascetics and Gendered Orders in Thailand* (NIAS Press, 2007).

John Strong, *The Buddha, A Short Biography* (OneWorld, 2001).

Maurice Walshe (translator), 'The Mahāpadāna Sutta', in *The Long Discourses of the Buddha: A Translation of the Dīgha Nikāya* (Wisdom Publications, 1987).

Paul Williams, *Buddhist Thought: A Complete Introduction to the Indian Tradition* (Routledge, 2000).

Paul Williams, *Mahāyāna Buddhism: The Doctrinal Foundations*, 2nd ed. (Routledge, 2009).

On the web

Kristin Barendsen, 'Joan Halifax: Fearless and Fragile', *Shambhala Sun*, May 2009. Available at: www.shambhalasun.com/index.php?option=content&task=view&id=3361 [last accessed 13 September 2013].

Berzin Archives, 'A summary report of the 2007 International Congress on Buddhist Women's Role in the Sangha'. Available at: www.berzinarchives.com/web/en/archives/approaching_buddhism/world_today/summary_report_2007_international_c/part_1.html [last accessed 13 September 2013].

Buddhanet, 'Outstanding Women in World Buddhism'. Available at: www.buddhanet.net/e-learning/history/women_world.htm [last accessed 13 September 2013].

José Cabezón, 'On the Ethics of the Tibetan Self-Immolations', *Religious Dispatches*, 16 June 2013. Available at: www.religiondispatches.org/archive/politics/7126/on_the_ethics_of_the_tibetan_self_immolations_/ [last accessed 13 September 2013].

Index

ALL THAT MATTERS: BUDDHISM

Author's profile

Pascale Engelmajer teaches Religious Studies at Carroll University in Wisconsin. She obtained her MA and PhD in Buddhist Studies from the University of Bristol. She lived in Thailand for several years, and has travelled extensively in Southeast Asia. She has also studied Buddhism and Buddhist meditation in several traditions, and one of her favourite pastimes is to visit Buddhist temples and centres wherever she lives. The other is to sample the food prepared by the communities that support these temples and centres. Her main academic interest focuses on the role of women in Buddhism and, in particular, on their spiritual path as described in the canonical literature. Her current projects include a revised version of her PhD thesis soon to be published, and research on immigrant Buddhist communities in Wisconsin.

Acknowledgements

Thanks are due to Professor Rupert Gethin for suggesting my name to George Miller and making this book possible. I am extremely thankful to Venerable Jinho and Chutima Maneewattana for their suggestion to consider vignettes on Venerable Chao Hwei and Khun Mae Siri respectively, for their help in obtaining information and for checking my descriptions. I also want to thank Justin Whitaker, Pascal Engelmajer and Massimo Rondolino for generously sharing their photographs with me. I am indebted to Amy Cropper, George Miller and Massimo Rondolino for reading drafts of this work and giving me invaluable feedback on very short notice. I further would like to thank my colleagues at Carroll University for welcoming my family and me at Carroll and making this first year in Wisconsin as comfortable as possible. Finally, my deepest gratitude to Max for his unfailing support and beautiful spirit.

Photo credits

Pascale F. Engelmajer (Fig. 0.3, 1.1 and 4.1); Justin Whitaker (Fig. 2.1, 2.2, 3.1, 3.2, 7.1, and 9.1); Massimo Rondolino (Fig. 4.2, 7.2 and 8.1; Pascal Engelmajer (Fig. 5.1); kallu, Flickr, reprinted under Creative Commons (Fig.6.1)

Maps courtesy of d-maps.com: http://d-maps.com/carte.php?num_car=55&lang=en (Fig. 0.1); http://d-maps.com/carte.php?num_car=3275&lang=en (Fig. 0.2)